A Preface to Paul

A Preface
to Paul

Morna D. Hooker

New York
OXFORD UNIVERSITY PRESS
1980

First published in Great Britain in 1979
under the title *Pauline Pieces*
by Epworth Press, The Methodist Publishing House,
Wellington Road, Wimbledon, London SW19 8EU

First published in the United States in 1980
by Oxford University Press, Inc., New York

Library of Congress Cataloging in Publication Data

Hooker, Morna Dorothy.
    A preface to Paul.

    Published in London in 1979 under title:
Pauline pieces.
    1. Bible. N.T. Epistles of Paul — Criticism,
interpretation, etc. I. Title.
BS2650.2.H66   1980   227′ .06   79-25658
ISBN 0-19-520195-7   ISBN 0-19-520188-4 pbk.

Printed in the United States of America

Contents

In grateful memory of my Father who helped with everything else I have written.

ONE

Through a Glass, Darkly

Whatever else St Paul may or may not have achieved, he
has certainly always succeeded in provoking strong reac-
tions. It seems that those who know anything at all about
him are either for him or against him; there are few who are
half-hearted in their response to him. His writings are
regarded as either boring or thrilling, too obscure to bother
with or so profound as to provide a constant source of
illumination. He himself is seen either as a conceited
trouble-maker or as the theologian to whom the Church
owes the greatest debt. Presumably anyone who reads
these words is likely to be among those who are predis-
posed to appreciate him, and will probably side with Tyn-
dale, who described Paul's writings as 'purest gospel' rather
than with those who have accused him of perverting the
gospel. But this is a charge which has often been brought
against Paul; again and again it has been said—'Jesus
preached one thing, the Church another'—and the finger of
accusation has pointed primarily at Paul. The recent controversy about *The Myth of God Incarnate*[1] has focused on
one aspect of an old problem, in which the role of Paul is
always crucial: to what extent is there continuity between
the message of Jesus and the faith of the Church?

To answer this question we need not only to pursue the
historical Jesus, but to understand the thought of Paul. The
fact that such very different answers are given is some
indication of the difficulties involved in doing either of
these things. I want to begin this study of St Paul by looking
at some of the reasons for the difficulties which arise in his
case. It is very tempting to begin by trying to say something
positive—but to do so might well give the misleading
impression that the evidence is straightforward. If what

[1] (Ed.) J. Hick (SCM 1977)

follows sounds negative, it is because I think it is important to note certain features which tend to twist the evidence, and must be noted as distorting factors. If I state the obvious, in pleading for caution in the way we handle the material, it is because too many dogmatic statements have been made about Paul on the basis of somewhat scanty evidence.

i) Paul gives us only a piecemeal picture of his theological position. Everything he wrote was occasional literature. Whether or not what we have is a sufficient sample to give us a fair picture of his thought depends to some extent on how many of the Pauline epistles we regard as authentic. But even if we accept the majority of the letters attributed to him as his, there are many aspects of Christian life about which Paul tells us little or nothing; like the visible section of an iceberg, his letters provide us with only part of his thinking. It is salutary also to remember that passages which have played a crucial part in the interpretation of Paul's theology, such as his discussion of resurrection in 1 Corinthians 15, and some which have played an important part in later theological debate—e.g. the famous Christ-hymn in Philippians 2—might easily *not* have survived. Had the cantankerous Corinthians torn up 1 Corinthians, for example, as perhaps they tore up an earlier letter from Paul, we should not today possess a great deal of what now seems vital information. As for Philippians 2, there are those who want to exclude this from the Pauline canon even now, on the grounds that Paul is using earlier material, or that the whole epistle was written by a later hand. Examples such as these make one wonder just how much of what Paul wrote has in fact survived, and how much of what we label 'Pauline' was in fact written by Paul; one wonders also what Paul might have written, had he known that later generations of Christians were going to hang on his words, and armies of research students analyse every tense and case that he used. Apart from Romans, Paul's letters were written to congregations who knew him and who had

8

heard him preach; they tend to fill in the gaps in their understanding of the gospel rather than start from the beginning. Reading them is rather like sitting in on a tutorial when a teacher goes over an essay with an undergraduate; there are some favourable comments on what has been well understood, but most of our time and attention is concentrated on points which have been misunderstood and mistakes which need to be put right. Trying to build up a picture of Paul's theology, then, is like trying to make a picture out of dots, such as one finds in children's drawing books; but in this case, we have not been supplied with any numbers to tell us the order in which to join the dots, and the resulting picture is somewhat distorted. We have only a sample of Paul's thought, and we do not know how representative that sample is. We do not even know how pure our sample is, since we cannot be sure precisely which of the letters attributed to Paul are in fact his own; at least some of them must be attributed to a later writer, but our problem is knowing which of the dubious ones we should include.

ii) My second difficulty arises from the fact that Paul's letters are occasional literature. It is the problem of knowing the extent to which the particular situation in which Paul found himself, and the particular situation of the community to which he was writing, have influenced not only what he chose to say, but the way in which he said it. The particular needs of a community—including their mistakes and their misunderstandings of the gospel as Paul understood it—are obviously important here. We should not know the Pauline tradition of the Last Supper, for example, if the Corinthians' behaviour at the eucharist had not seemed to Paul to be scandalous. But has his interpretation of the eucharist, which links it closely with the death of Jesus, been stressed in this passage precisely because of their misunderstanding? Would he perhaps have given a different interpretation in a different situation? Has his own interpretation perhaps developed in reaction to the

9

Corinthians' unseemly behaviour? And to what extent have Paul's own experiences and problems influenced what he writes? We need to consider the situation of Paul himself as well as the situation of the communities to which he was writing. We must all be aware of the way in which our own experiences influence what we write. Any preacher worth his salt who looks back through his file of old sermons will be reminded of past events; some passages will link immediately with particular events in the experience of the congregation; but others will link up with particular events in the preacher's own life—with experiences of tragedy and joy, with books which have left an impact, with incidents of one kind and another; if they do not, then they will have been poor sermons! The best are always written out of the preacher's own experience. Paul's letters were surely influenced by contemporary events in a similar way; each of them reflects his thinking at a particular stage of his life, as he responded to a particular situation. Paul's theology was no more static than Paul himself, and in reading his letters we are reading theology in the making. If we try to make them into a systematic structure, we may well distort his teaching; Paul is essentially a practical theologian.

iii) The third difficulty is also linked with the situation of Paul and the communities to which he wrote, and concerns the role played by the opposition in the composition of his letters. It is clear that in many of them Paul is arguing against alternative interpretations of the gospel (or perhaps false gospels), and that he is in turn defending himself against attack and attacking those who oppose him. Just at present it is fashionable to find opponents lurking not only behind every epistle but behind every gospel as well—as though nobody ever wrote anything except to refute the views of someone else. This is surely an exaggeration; New Testament scholars seem to be thinking of the composition of the books of the New Testament in terms of a debate between German theologians! It is a distortion to suggest that Paul was incapable of writing except to contradict what others had said. Nevertheless, there clearly were some who were opposed to Paul and his gospel. The problem of identifying these opponents is, however, a difficult one. Were they Jews? Jewish Christians? Judaizing Gentile Christians? Gnostics? Was there one group, or more than one? The decision we make as to when Paul is attacking opponents, and the seriousness which we ascribe to the rift between them and Paul, and the label which we give to them—these are all factors which will influence the way in which we interpret what Paul himself writes. For opposition would inevitably influence what Paul wrote to his churches, and would cause him to emphasize certain ideas and themes. But opposition may have done more than influence the way in which he formulated his thinking; it may have had a formative influence on his ideas—may have led him to develop his ideas in certain directions. It has often been said that heresy was the crucible of Christology; whether we can speak of heresy or not at this period is debatable—probably not; that is something which comes later. But the beliefs of those who opposed Paul may well have had a significant influence on the development of his Christological thought—even if it was only in a negative way, in making him express his understanding of the truth in other ways.

iv) All the New Testament writers—with the exception only of James—are so Christocentric in their thinking as to have what is almost an obsession with Christology. 'Obsession' is perhaps not quite the right word, but what I mean is that their attention is focused wholly on the figure of Christ; it is he who is the new factor in the situation—and God is taken for granted. Naturally enough, writers explore primarily Christological themes, and they assume a background of theological knowledge, even when they are writing to Gentile readers. Their concern is to relate what they have come to believe about Christ to the theological insights that they already had; they concentrate, therefore, on Christology, on the figure of Jesus Christ. But at a later period, when the New Testament itself has become normative, and the basis of doctrine, it is arguable that there is something of an imbalance. Certainly it needs to be set against a knowledge of the Old Testament and of Jewish religious practice. To concentrate attention on the New Testament alone is to concentrate on that which made the first Christians different from their Jewish contemporaries and to ignore what they had in common. Indeed, a distortion often arises because it is forgotten that most—if not all—of the New Testament was written from within the context of Judaism. I suspect that we tend to underestimate the Jewishness of the New Testament. The antithesis which we naturally make between Jew and Christian is foreign to Paul: for him the natural antithesis is Jew and Gentile. For him, Christianity is the true fulfiment of Judaism, which paradoxically embraces Gentiles. The position of the early Christians must have been in some ways similar to that of the early Methodists in this country—still within the Anglican fold (in their own eyes, at least), but gradually finding themselves excluded from the parent body. Nevertheless for many years individual Methodists continued to worship in the parish church and to attend Methodist services as well: their Methodism was complementary to Anglican traditions—not in contradiction with it. This pattern continued in Cornwall until the middle of the nineteenth century. My own great, great grandfather—who came of good Anglican stock—used to worship in the parish church of St Just-in-Roseland on Sunday mornings, and in the evenings would take his tuning-fork to 'raise the tunes' at the service in the Methodist chapel. It is said that he used to meet the Rector on the way, who greeted him with the words 'Good evening Mr Hooker; you're going to the devil's house again I see'. It is not surprising that the break between Anglicans and Methodists finally came about; but with it there came an impoverishment of Methodism, since it lost part of its heritage—the liturgy of the Anglican Church—and retained that which distinguished it from the parent community—namely the non-conformist preaching service. I suspect that the break between Christianity and Judaism, when it came at the end of the first century AD, also meant that Christianity lost a large part of its Jewish flavour, which had at first been taken as read. It is important, then, to remember Paul's Jewish background and assumptions; those interpreters who have made him into a Hellenistic thinker have perhaps forgotten the part of Paul's theology which he did not need to stress.

v) We shall certainly distort Paul if we forget that his beliefs were inevitably expressed in terms and forms belonging to the pattern of thought which he inherited. Whether or not it is possible to extract ideas from the particular forms in which they are expressed and to restate them in modern terms is a matter of considerable debate. Some New Testament terms quickly lost their meaning when Christianity moved out of its Jewish context. One can see this happening even within the New Testament. The term 'the Son of man', for example, an odd phrase in Greek, soon became a conundrum and was abandoned by the Church. At a later period it had to be given a meaning because it was a part of scripture; some explanation of this odd phrase, used so often in the gospels, had to be found; so it was taken to mean the humanity of Christ. There is no agreement among scholars today as to what this term means, but at least one can safely say that, whatever else it may mean, it does not mean that! The term 'Messiah' was equally enigmatic to non-Jews. But here a different process took place. The term was adopted as a name. For Paul to say that Jesus was the Messiah was a meaningful statement; it expressed his understanding of the role of Jesus; it summed up the idea of the fulfilment of God's purposes; it focused attention on Jesus as the one through whom God was at work. But by the time the gospel moved into the Hellenistic world, the term was already meaningless. Surprisingly, one can still find those who ignore this loss of meaning, and seem to assume that it will make a

13

meaningful impact on those who read or hear it—even those outside the Jewish or Christian communities. Cycling down the Woodstock Road in North Oxford one day I found myself confronted by a lurid poster which declared: 'Jesus said: I am the Christ'. My first reaction was to retort: 'According to the gospels he made no such direct claim'; my second was to say: 'So what?' What were the inhabitants of North Oxford expected to make of this statement? Unless they already had some Christian commitment, how were they expected to understand it? The claim that Jesus is the Messiah—the Christ—makes sense only within a particular culture.

vi) So we come to the limitation placed upon us by our lack of evidence—a lack of evidence not only about Paul himself and about his situation, but about first-century Judaism in general, and about the theological position of Paul's Christian contemporaries. Our knowledge in these areas is so partial that we are bound to distort Paul's own thought and to misunderstand the background out of which he came. It is because of these gaps in our knowledge that scholars are able to give such widely differing interpretations of Paul—seeing him, for example, as a Hebrew of Hebrews on the one hand, or as profoundly influenced by Hellenistic thought on the other. The discovery of the Dead Sea Scrolls was a healthy reminder of how little we know about first-century Judaism. Confident remarks about what was and was not possible within first-century Judaism were proved false by those discoveries. But the fact that we now know a great deal more about that period should not beguile us into falling into the same trap again. The discovery of this material was due to chance, just as its preservation was due to chance; it is still only a portion of the evidence we need to recreate a complete picture; we do not know how typical it is—probably it is eccentric, and so of little help in telling us about the great majority of Palestinian Jews in general; the beliefs of this sectarian group may or may not be of help in our search for the background of Christian thought. It is always tempting to use the few pieces of evidence which one has, to make a comprehensible picture; but the vital pieces of information may well be missing.

vii) Another factor which may distort our understanding arises out of our own situation. If Paul's interpretation of Christ was conditioned by his experience and culture and thought patterns, so too is ours. We automatically give to words the value which they have for us. One result of this is that Christians tend to read the New Testament through Chalcedonian spectacles. An interesting example of this has been highlighted by the recent controversy about *The Myth of God Incarnate*. It is clear that many Christians give to the term 'Son of God' the full value that it has in later Christological statements—whereas it probably had a very different significance in the New Testament. It is very difficult to put ourselves back into Paul's shoes—but it is equally difficult to take off our own—to shed our knowledge of later events and developments.

A few years ago I went on my first visit to Africa, and spent three months in Ghana. Before I went, I tried to learn all I could about that country; I read books and articles, asked friends who had lived there innumerable questions, watched various features on television. Theoretically I knew a great deal about the country—but I still found it difficult to imagine it. And when I actually arrived there, the impact that it made upon me was overwhelming. I can well imagine that anyone making the transition in the opposite direction would experience an even greater shock. However good our information may be, the experience itself still makes an amazing impact on us. I have no doubt that a visit back in time to the first century, were such a thing possible, would be an even more overwhelming experience; we may think we possess a great deal of information about life then—but it is quite impossible for us to put ourselves into the skins of first-century men and women.

There was another feature about my visit to Ghana which seems to me relevant to this discussion. In spite of being plunged into a very different culture from my own—especially in the north of that country—it was impossible for me to forget that at the end of my visit, an aeroplane built in a highly technological society would whisk me back to the familiar sights and sounds of England. I found it impossible to take off my twentieth-century spectacles or to interpret my experiences except in relation to my own cultural values. It is very difficult indeed to become immersed in another culture to the extent that one ceases to judge it from the standpoint of one's own. It was this difficulty which led to many mistakes on the part of missionaries, going from one cultural setting to another. I suggest that it has also led to many misinterpretations of the New Testament: we find it impossible to interpret it except in relation to our own experiences.

Another way in which modern attitudes influence our understanding of Paul is seen in the assumption that the apostle must have thought out a consistent theological position. It is certainly true that Paul applied his own logic to theological questions, and that we can study him building up an argument from premise to conclusion. But just as we may find that his starting point is often very different from our own, and that his method of argument is strange to us (since it is usually typical of a first-century Jewish rabbi), so too we may discover that his conclusions do not necessarily cohere consistently with other ideas into a theological structure. What looks consistent to us may not have seemed consistent to him—and vice versa. It may even be that what we understand by consistency was a foreign notion to him. It is possible, for example, that the modern tendency to analyse Paul's letters into collections of fragments from several letters on the basis that he appears to contradict himself or change course abruptly is the result of trying to assess Paul by a modern tool which is here inappropriate.

viii) My final danger is what I call the distortion of the

canon. We have, I imagine, all become accustomed to the notion that a significant shift in thought took place at the resurrection. Whatever position we may take up regarding the relationship between the historical Jesus and the Christ of faith, and the degree of continuity between them, there is no denying that Jesus seen through the eyes of resurrection faith looks very different from Jesus 'according to the flesh'—to borrow a Pauline phrase. The resurrection is the point at which Jesus becomes the interpreted rather than the interpreter—the one who is proclaimed rather than the one who proclaims. We are perhaps less aware of a somewhat similar shift regarding the New Testament itself— when these documents in turn changed from being active interpreters and became interpreted. The canonization of Paul's epistles meant that they became the basis of later doctrinal systems—a far remove from their original purpose. It is perhaps not surprising if no good theology of Paul has ever been written; he himself did not set out to write systematic theology, and to use occasional literature as the basis of a system must inevitably distort it. What happened was that Paul's thought was in effect fossilized. It was taken as valid and authentic teaching for all periods of the Church after him. The way in which Paul's thought was distorted as a result is perhaps most obvious in the matter of practical advice which he gave regarding particular ethical situations, which were then taken as obligatory commands by later generations. The most ludicrous example is seen in the matter of women wearing hats in church. Because it seemed to Paul (conditioned as he was by his Jewish upbringing) that the only way of avoiding scandal in the particular social conditions of first-century Corinth was for women to wear something on their heads in public, women continued to be expected to wear hats in church for almost 1900 years thereafter. Could there have been a greater distortion of the spirit of Paul, who insisted that religion was not a matter of law, than to turn him into a great lawgiver? Paul's own method in dealing with ethical

17

questions was to apply theological first principles; but his judgments in particular situations were turned into a set of rules by the fossilization of the canon.

It is arguable that in some ways Paul's Christology was also 'occasional'. For he uses a variety of images and ideas—influenced sometimes by his Old Testament background, sometimes by the particular situation which he is addressing. Sometimes, perhaps, he takes over terms which are used by those with whom he disagrees and adapts them. If we try to reduce all this to a nice neat system and to analyse it in detail, we shall surely distort Paul. It may be, too, that to take ideas out of particular contexts and assume that they are central and essential to his theological thought is equally misleading. To speak of Jesus as Wisdom, for example, meant something very specific within the particular context of Hellenistic Jewish thought; to build a Christology around that statement is to erect a system upon an image. It may be that the same thing has been done in the case of Paul's image of the Christian community as the body of Christ; was the idea quite as central and important for Paul himself as later theological developments might suggest?

One result of making the New Testament the basis of a system is that we tend to expect it to answer our questions, and forget that it was meant to answer the questions of those to whom and by whom it was written. The extent to which it is proper to expect the New Testament to answer our questions at all is another question—though an important and vital one. But certainly it is very easy for us to impose our patterns of thought unconsciously on the material. As an example of this, let us return to the problem of the relationship between the Jesus of history and the Christ of faith with which we began. It is often said that Paul had no interest in the historical Jesus, that he was concerned only with the Christ of faith. Bultmann, true to the Lutheran principle of *sola fide*, appeals to 2 Corinthians 5:16, where Paul rejects knowledge of Christ according to the

flesh, in support of his understanding of Paul as deliber-
ately rejecting knowledge of the historical Jesus as the basis
of faith. References to Jesus are strangely wanting in the
Pauline epistles; it is his death, not his life, which is significant. Other scholars protest that this is an exaggeration;
there are in fact references to the birth and life of Jesus
(though in very general terms); and there are occasional
quotations—or at least echoes—of the words of Jesus. I
wonder, however, whether to discuss the question at this
level is not to ask the question in our terms—to look for, or
to notice the absence of, evidence of a kind that we
consider significant. The lack of references to the earthly
life of Jesus does not necessarily mean that Paul has no
interest in the historical Jesus and has based his theology on
the myth of a descending Redeemer. I find it salutory here
to compare Paul's letters with 1 John, which begins with a
reference to that which we have heard and which we have
seen with our eyes and touched with our hands, but which
makes no use of tradition about the historical Jesus
—though if 1 John is from the same stable as the Fourth
Gospel (let alone from the same author) the writer
must have known such traditions. Perhaps the difference
between the literary forms of epistle and gospel does, after
all, make a difference to the material which is included.
Apparent theological differences could be due to different
literary methods. We must not misuse the evidence by
forcing it to answer our questions.

But neither must we misinterpret the character of the
evidence. There is an obvious shift in perspective between
Jesus and Paul, caused by the resurrection. Inevitably, the
teaching of Paul centres on Jesus himself and on what God
has done through him. His gospel is not the gospel which
Jesus himself taught; it is a gospel *about* Jesus Christ. But
we do well to remember that this is true also of the evangelists, even when they report the teaching and actions of
Jesus. This is something quite independent of the question
of the use of 'historical' material. Paul may well have been

19

interested in what we term the Jesus of history, without making much use of material about him in his epistles; it is also possible that the evangelists used apparently 'historical' material for entirely theological purposes. Their method is different from Paul's, but they make it as plain as he does that the activity of God is focused in Jesus, and that salvation comes through him; Jesus himself may teach about God—but the attention of the evangelists is centred on Jesus. By their arrangement of the material, the vital question which faces the reader throughout is the response which we make to Jesus himself. We must look for continuity, then, not in any historical interest in Jesus on the part of Paul, nor in any identity in the content of their preaching, but in more subtle ways.

What I have said in this chapter has perhaps seemed entirely negative. You may perhaps have guessed that it would be so from my title, and since I am convinced that the great need is to proceed with caution, I am unrepentant. In future chapters, we shall try to see how much we can in fact discover about Paul's understanding of the gospel.

TWO

Christ our Righteousness

In the last chapter we looked at the difficulties of saying anything at all about Paul: for one reason or another it seems inevitable that we shall distort his meaning and misunderstand his words. You may well be wondering whether we have not reached an impasse! Can we say anything at all about Paul's theological position? Can we unearth his understanding of the gospel, or discover what was, for him, the heart of the gospel? And did he differ in his teaching from what the other apostles were saying? Fortunately, we have, if not *the* answer, at least *an* answer from Paul himself, for in writing to the Corinthian Christians he found it necessary to remind them of the gospel which he had preached to them, and which he fears they may be forsaking. He writes[1]:

'My brothers, I must remind you of the gospel that I preached to you; the gospel which you received, on which you have taken your stand, and which is now bringing you salvation. Do you still hold fast the Gospel as I preached it to you? If not, your conversion was in vain. First and foremost, I handed on to you the facts which had been imparted to me: that Christ died for our sins, in accordance with the scriptures; that he was buried; that he was raised to life on the third day, according to the scriptures; and that he appeared to Cephas, and afterwards to the Twelve. . . .'

After he had appeared to various other witnesses, then, 'in the end he appeared even to me'.

The 'facts' of the gospel, as Paul gives them here, are summed up in four verbs: Christ died, he was buried, he was raised, he was seen. We can, indeed, reduce them to two, for the phrase 'he was buried' serves to confirm the

[1] Corinthians 15:1–5, N.E.B.

21

reality of the death, just as the words 'he was seen' confirm the reality of the resurrection. He died; he was raised; this is the basis of the gospel. 'I decided to know nothing among you,' Paul tells them, 'except Christ and him crucified'. But not only crucified—for 'if Christ was not raised, then our gospel is null and void, and so is your faith'. This, says Paul, is the gospel which is bringing the Corinthians salvation. But can we really reduce Paul's gospel to the simple statement that Christ died and was raised? It may be, as I suggested previousely, that Paul's summary here is influenced by the particular situation to which he is writing; perhaps he has selected these statements in writing to the Corinthians because he is dealing with their questions about the resurrection of the dead. Let us try a passage in Romans, where Paul again sums up the gospel, 'the word of faith which we proclaim: if on your lips is the confession, "Jesus is Lord", and in your heart the faith that God raised him from the dead, then you will find salvation'.[2] Once again, faith in the gospel means the acknowledgement that God raised Christ from the dead, but this time we are told also that the confession that Jesus is Lord is a way of expressing this belief in his resurrection. Again, in Romans, we are told that the gospel is 'about God's Son, who was descended from David according to the flesh, but designated Son of God in power according to the Spirit of holiness by the resurrection from the dead, Jesus Christ our Lord'.[3] This summary of the gospel is a little more elaborate, but notice how, once again, the resurrection is central, and how it is *through* the resurrection that Jesus is acknowledged as Son of God and Lord.

There is no reason to disbelieve Paul when he tells us that this was the gospel which he received. As far as we can tell from the New Testament, the rest of the Church would have agreed with these summaries; indeed, it may well be that the summaries are not Paul's own, but were widely

[2] Romans 10:9
[3] Romans 1:3 f.

22

used in the early Church. But if Paul's gospel was really so simple, how is it that the epistles are so full of theological obscurity? And if Paul preached the same gospel as other Christians, how is it that he so often seemed to be in disagreement with them? For the Paul who emerges from the epistles does seem very often to be at loggerheads with someone: and though I argued in the previous chapter that we must not assume that Paul is *always* opposing someone else, it has to be admitted that he does frequently appear to be engaged in dispute of one kind or another, attacking those who disagree with him and upholding the truth of 'his' gospel against the views of others. It is for this reason, perhaps, that many people regard Paul as a somewhat disagreeable little man, who spent his time rushing around the ancient world, laying down the law, blowing his own trumpet, and haranguing his converts about justification by faith.

But is this 'simple' gospel quite so simple after all? What did it mean for Paul to preach that Christ had died and that God had raised him? Paul was a Jew: it is very easy to overlook the implications of this obvious fact. It was no simple message for Paul to declare that the Christ, the Jewish Messiah, had died, that he had indeed been crucified. In 1 Corinthians Paul describes the very idea of a crucified Messiah as 'a stumbling-block to the Jews'.[4] The conviction that it was the Messiah who had been crucified meant that he had to rethink all his ideas about God and about his own relationship with God. What sort of a God was it who acted in this kind of way, who permitted the Messiah's death? That he had indeed acted in this way was proved for Paul beyond all doubt by the resurrection: it was by the power of God that Christ had been raised from death. And so Paul, who had previously thought that his relationship with God was a matter of his own scrupulous obedience to the Law, found that he had to make room in his thought and life for a crucified Messiah whom God had raised from the dead. But this teaching was not only

[4] 1 Corinthians 1:23

23

a stumbling-block to Jews: it was dismissed as utter foolishness by non-Jews, too. Men naturally associate God with glory and power: what, then, was this talk of the Son of God dying in shame and weakness? The simple message of Christ crucified and risen has far-reaching implications. What some of those implications are we see in the epistles, where we find Paul hammering out the meaning of his gospel in a variety of different situations.

But what about the controversy over justification by grace through faith? Might it not be argued that this was an unnecessary Pauline elaboration of the 'simple' gospel that Christ died and was raised? On the contrary, it seems to me to be the logical interpretation of Christ's death and resurrection within the particular context of the Jewish understanding of God's Law and the character of righteousness. It is in Galatians, in particular, that we find Paul insisting that the grace of God in Christ is alone sufficient for man's salvation, and fulminating against the suggestion that non-Jewish Christians should be asked to accept the Jewish rite of circumcision and to keep the regulations of the Jewish Law. Why does Paul get so hot under the collar over this question? What harm could there be in Gentile Christians following the example of their Jewish Christian brothers, who apparently continued to follow the regulations about food and ritual cleanliness? Why should they not express their acceptance of God's plan of salvation, which had come to its fulfilment in Christ, by complying with the requirements of the Jewish Law? In order to understand Paul's teaching about justification by grace through faith, we need to realize its crucial relevance to the critical situation existing in the Galatian churches. A group of teachers, either Jewish Christians or Gentile converts who have embraced Judaism as well as Christianity, have apparently disturbed the Galatian Christians by suggesting that Paul's own teaching was deficient. This fact they explained by maintaining that Paul himself was not a true apostle, since he was not a member of the original

Jerusalem hierarchy; he had not taught them the whole gospel. These teachers urged that baptism into Christ was only the first step on the way to salvation; the next was the acceptance of the Jewish rite of circumcision, and the obedience to the regulations of the Jewish Law which that involved. Paul reacted in a way that may well have seemed to many of his Christian contemporaries unnecessarily and absurdly violent. Such teachers, he declares, 'distort the gospel of Christ', and they will be punished accordingly. The Galatians must on no account accept circumcision, for to do so would be to cut themselves off from Christ. 'You can take it from me,' he writes, 'that every man who receives circumcision is under obligation to keep the entire law. When you seek to be justified by way of law, your relation with Christ is completely severed: you have fallen out of the domain of God's grace.'

We may perhaps be tempted to sympathize with the Galatians, and to ask whether Paul is not making a great deal of fuss about something rather unimportant. Later on, Paul himself declares that 'if we are in Christ, circumcision makes no difference at all'. One might have supposed, then, that the logical thing for him to say to the Galatians was 'Of course you need not be circumcised, because it can make *no difference* to the relationship which you already have with Christ. Circumcision is an optional and unnecessary extra.' Instead, we find him saying 'You *must not* be circumcised, because circumcision will cut you off from Christ.'

Paul's teaching here is controlled by a deeper logic; it is grounded in his understanding of the basic facts of the gospel by which men are saved—Christ died, and has been raised. It is also, I suspect, influenced by his own experience, for the complete antithesis here between law and grace reflects his own dramatic conversion from Judaism to Christianity. Brought up a strict Pharisee, Paul had devoted his early life to keeping the Jewish Law, his one aim being to earn God's approval by his own righteousness. As a Christian, Paul had discovered that the right relationship with God which he had tried for so long to deserve was offered to him freely by God's grace. He was forced to admit that the Law he had obeyed for so long had condemned as a criminal the one whom he now acknowledged as Messiah. There could be only one conclusion for Paul: the Law was *not* the way to salvation. It had failed by its very nature. For the attempt to keep it had turned men's minds in upon themselves instead of on God, caused them to seek their own righteousness instead of accepting God's, made them rely on their own activity, and blinded them to the activity of God. For Paul, the Law now symbolized the effort to achieve salvation by one's own efforts. This was why he was so adamant about the Galatians' desire to become Jews; for it was an attempt to earn salvation, and to rely upon their own 'merit' instead of trusting in God. For a Christian, this was a retrograde step; it was a return to self-reliance, and so a denial of the grace of God. Salvation is freely offered to man in the 'simple' gospel that Jesus died and was raised.

Against this background, we can understand why Paul says what he does in writing to the Galatians. We understand, for example, why he begins in a somewhat pompous way: 'From Paul, an apostle, not by human appointment or human commission, but by commission from Jesus Christ and from God the Father who raised him from the dead.' We understand why he continues for paragraph after paragraph to emphasize his authority as an apostle, and his independence from other Christian leaders. It is not because he wants honour or privilege for himself—though that is how his words have come across to those who have read them without appreciating the situation with which he is dealing. It is because his authority as an apostle has been challenged—and with it the gospel he has preached. He must establish his position as an apostle in order to establish the validity of 'his' gospel. He is fighting for the truth of the gospel—that man cannot 'earn' or merit salvation, but is saved by the grace of God alone. 'If righteousness comes by law, then Christ died for nothing.'[5] The death of Christ makes nonsense of any idea that man can save himself by his own efforts. No wonder that Paul cried in exasperation: 'You stupid Galatians! You must have been bewitched— you before whose eyes Jesus Christ was openly displayed upon his cross!'[6]

But was Paul right? If he was, then the average Englishman's understanding of Christianity is wrong. For most people still believe in salvation by works; they assume that the Christian is the man or woman who tries to live a decent moral life, goes to church on Sundays, and hopes that his or her good deeds will be chalked up in some heavenly account. For Paul, this is an utter distortion of the gospel: good works are never 'ours' to present to God, but are the result of our life in Christ; they are never our achievement, but only his achievement in us. To forget that for a moment is in Paul's view to make the death of Christ meaningless.

But is was not only these fanatics for the Jewish Law with whom Paul had trouble. In Corinth he ran up against another group of men—this time with a taste for philosophy; they, too, in Paul's eyes, were in danger of undermining the gospel. Paul himself admits that these men could put rings round him in public debate, and make his 'simple' message of the gospel look rather foolish. His objection to their teaching was that they, too, were trying to 'add' something to the gospel—and by doing so were, in fact, destroying it. These men wanted to add, not the Jewish Law, but 'wisdom'. What exactly this wisdom was is by no means clear, but it seems to have been an elaborate 'explanation' of the Christian faith in terms of Greek philosophy. Once again, Paul's account of the gospel was being regarded as inadequate; something more than simple faith in Christ was needed. Although it was expressed in different terms, the danger in Corinth was basically the same as in Galatia; for it

[5] Galatians 2:21
[6] Galatians 3:1

was a temptation to rely upon oneself—upon one's own cleverness, ability, intellect. This is why, in writing to the Corinthians, Paul contrasts his own message of the crucified Christ with the search for wisdom which can empty the Cross of all meaning. This is why he declares that the apparent folly and weakness of God, seen in the Cross, are wiser and stronger than the wisdom and strength of men, whose efforts can never earn them salvation. 'There is no place,' he writes, 'for pride in the presence of God. You are in Christ Jesus by God's act, for God has made him our wisdom; he is our righteousness'.[7] If Christ is our wisdom and our righteousness, it is folly indeed to look any further.

Paul speaks in Galatians in terms of law and grace, and in 1 Corinthians in terms of wisdom and folly: but the fundamental antithesis in both epistles is between self-reliance and reliance upon God; between pride in one's own achievements and trust in the achievements of God; between a life which is focused on oneself, and a life which is centred upon God. This contrast is fundamental because it is grounded in the gospel itself. Christ died; confronted with the humility and weakness of God, what place can there be for pride or human confidence?

In these two letters, both of them by Paul—and nobody has seriously questioned the authenticity of either Galatians or 1 Corinthians—we have what seem at first to be totally different ways of talking about the gospel. Yet when we tease out the meaning of the different passages, we see that Paul's basic theological position is the same in them both: it is the same understanding of the gospel of Christ's death and resurrection which causes him to react in the way he does in writing to these different groups of Christians; the differences in expression and vocabulary are very largely explained by the different situations with which he is dealing.

It is a popular belief that Paul's understanding of the

[7] 1 Corinthians 1:29 f.

gospel could best be summed up in the phrase 'justification by faith.' It is certainly true that Luther saw this as the core of the Pauline gospel. Paul himself, I think, might have wanted to put it rather differently. For one thing, I think he would have preferred the phrase 'justification by grace through faith'; what he opposes to man's attempt to justify himself by the works of the Law is the free grace of God. But secondly, as we have already seen, 'justification by grace through faith' is really only one way of expressing his understanding of the basic gospel of Christ's death and resurrection. It was the interpretation which brought out the significance of that gospel in a Jewish context—the context which was the most normal one for Paul himself and for many of his converts. For Paul, the acceptance of Jesus as God's Messiah had meant not only the recognition that Jesus was the fulfilment of everything that the Law had promised; it had meant also the acknowledgement of the inadequacy of the Law as a way of life. In one sense Jesus had fulfilled the Law—but in another he had replaced it. He had replaced it as the way of being in a right relationship with God: the Law had failed to give Paul the righteousness which it demanded; this righteousness he found given to him by his relationship with Christ. Jesus had replaced the Law also in being the way of life for those who were in a right relationship with God; instead of living in accordance with the precepts of the Law, Paul now lived 'in Christ'. For the Jewish people, the Law was seen as the fence which surrounded them, marking them off from other nations as God's holy people; it was the Law which offered them righteousness, and so life. For Paul, righteousness was no longer to be found in the Law, but in Christ. The proof of this was to be seen in the resurrection, for in raising Christ from death—a death which had brought him under the condemnation of the Law—God had declared Christ to be innocent, righteous; he had, to use technical vocabulary, justified him. The idea that Jesus himself is 'justified' by God is rarely spelt out by Paul, but it is essential to his whole understanding of justification. He sees the

29

resurrection as a great act of vindication, in which God reverses the verdict which had condemned Jesus to death, and proclaims his righteousness. It is this initial act of vindication, the justification of Jesus himself, on which the justification of Christians depends. Those who identify themselves with his death and resurrection can share in his death to sin and his declaration of righteousness: they share in his status of being righteous before God—an idea which is summed up well in a line from a hymn by William Bright: 'And only look on us as found in Him'.[8]

Paul draws such a strong contrast between life under the Law and Life in Christ that it sometimes seems as though he were suggesting that the Law itself is evil. This, of course, is not so. The Law was given by God himself, and is therefore good and holy. It is the power of sin, which has invaded the world through the sin of man, which has prevented the Law doing what it promised; through the power of sin, the Law itself has become an alien power holding man in slavery. What was in itself good has been used for evil. The Law points to what is good, but is incapable of making men good. It is in this situation of impasse that God has made Christ our righteousness.

Paul's quarrel with the Law is therefore a limited one, though a supremely important one: it concerns its inability to make men righteous. In all other ways, Paul reveres the Law—as the revelation of God's character, as the account of the demands he made on his people, and as the witness to Christ. We may well doubt whether Luke represents Paul correctly in Acts when he portrays him as scrupulous in his adherence to the Law; but it is perhaps significant that Luke does not regard Paul as an iconoclast. To one, at least, of his most ardent admirers, Paul did not appear as being in any way opposed to the Law.

For Paul, the Law fails because it allows man to attempt his own justification. In contrast, he stresses the activity of God himself. But how does man become the recipient of

[8] *Methodist Hymn Book* 759

30

God's grace? What is the faith by which man responds, and how is it obtained? For Paul, it is clear that faith and the works of the Law are mutually exclusive: faith is the very opposite of reliance on one's own righteousness, for it is an acceptance of the gift of righteousness offered by God. The believer needs to do nothing except believe—and even that is not to be understood as a requirement; rather it is simply the response to God's grace. Faith is trust in the trustworthiness of God, and leads in turn to one's own faithfulness—that is to obedience; its implications are summed up neatly in a line from an old-fashioned hymn: 'Trust and obey'.

Paul's understanding of faith as trust in God is often contrasted with a view of faith as an intellectual belief that certain things are true. This is a valid contrast, provided we remember that for Paul faith in God and faith in Christ imply certain beliefs about the activity of God in the past and a confident assurance that he can be trusted to act in a consistent way in the future: faith inevitably involves an acknowledgment of God's activity in Christ. This is why we find him placing the verbs 'confess' and 'believe' in parallelism in Romans 10:9: 'if you confess with your lips that Jesus is Lord and believe in your heart that God raised him from the dead, you will be saved.' The sign of faith and the occasion for confession would no doubt have been baptism: but baptism was itself something more, since it was the identification of the believer with the death and resurrection of Christ, and with the verdicts of condemnation and vindication pronounced upon him.

But if we allow Paul's argument that men and women are justified by grace and not by works, through Christ and not through the Law, we are still left with the question: How is this achieved? How can the death and resurrection of Christ make men and women righteous in the sight of God? It is important to recognize that Paul does not give any *one* answer to this question. He uses a variety of images to express it, and we shall be exploring some of these in the

31

next chapter. For the moment we may note that the way in which justification is centred in Pauline thought on the death and resurrection of Christ brings us back to the perennial problem of the relationship between Jesus and Paul. In one sense it is obvious that Jesus preached one thing and Paul another. But did Paul 'pervert' the religion of Jesus, as some have claimed? Or can we trace a continuity between the preaching of Jesus and that of Paul? Those who attempt to answer this question usually concentrate on the problem of the so-called messianic self-consciousness of Jesus and the use of Christological titles by Paul and other early Christian teachers. Did Jesus think of himself as Messiah at all? Did he use the enigmatic phrase 'the Son of man' to describe his own role? Is there a justifiable continuity between Jesus' own understanding of his role and the faith of the early Church? I would like to approach the question in another way, by thinking instead about the relationship between Paul's understanding of the gospel, as we tried to uncover it, and the message of Jesus.

As far as Jesus himself is concerned, there seems to be general agreement—in spite of the problems involved in recovering his teaching—that his message was focused, not on himself, but on the Kingdom of God. Discussion of this theme by New Testament scholars has concentrated on the problem of the time of its coming: is the Kingdom here or is it not? The Kingdom is an eschatological concept—but are we dealing with future eschatology, realized eschatology, or perhaps inaugurated eschatology? The scholarly jargon is an attempt to explain a tension in the sayings of Jesus: there is a sense in which the Kingdom has come in the activity of Jesus, and a sense in which it is obviously not yet here. It is worth noting that we find precisely the same tension in what Paul says about justification. Being acknowledged as righteous in the sight of God is something which belongs to the End—like the Kingdom, it is an eschatological concept. Paradoxically, this declaration of righteousness has been brought into the present; men and women have been made righteous already in Christ, and already experience a relationship of being right with God. The person of Jesus has brought the eschatological experience into the present. Yet the full enjoyment of that experience lies in the future. In both Jesus' proclamation of the Kingdom, and Paul's teaching about righteousness, the final action of God is seen as already present, focused in the figure of Jesus—and yet still to be completed in the future. The difference between Jesus' declaration of the Kindom and Paul's preaching of justification is that for Jesus the action is centred on his ministry, and for Paul, on Christ's death and resurrection.

A second link between these two concepts of the Kingdom and justification is to be seen in the fact that both of them are basically concerned with the relationship between God and man. Both involve a process of judgment, which necessarily involves a negative as well as a positive aspect; but both of them are about the restoration of a relationship which God intended to exist. Scholars have tended to stress the so-called 'apocalyptic' aspect of the Kingdom, and have forgotten that it is not just a cataclysmic event, but the inauguration of the rule of God. In the gospels, those who follow Jesus are promised a share in the Kingdom; for Paul, those who join themselves to Christ share in the relationship with God which he enjoys.

Another aspect of the Kingdom which is often overlooked is its ethical aspect. God cannot rule in a vacuum. Jesus' ethical teaching is not an interim measure or an accidental by-product. If God rules, men must obey—and their obedience is seen in their love for him and for their neighbour. Just as New Testament scholars do not always seem to know what to do with Jesus' ethical teaching, and how to fit it into the coming of the Kingdom, so they often are not sure what to do with Paul's ethical teaching, and how to fit that into this teaching about justification. I suggest that in each case there is a logical link between gospel and ethics, between the good news of salvation, and God's demands. The right relationship of man with God which is brought about by belonging to the Kingdom or by being justified in Christ must inevitably be expressed in right behaviour; those who belong to the Kingdom, those who belong to Christ, must live according to what they are.

Can we find continuity between Jesus and Paul? Did Paul teach a totally different gospel? Of course there are differences between them. It would be absurd to suggest that we can simply equate Jesus' teaching on the Kingdom of God with Paul's on justification. Recent New Testament theology has properly reacted against the tendency to assume that all biblical writers are really saying the same thing, and that all differences between them can be blurred. The present tendency is to sort the material into different pigeon holes and to stress the differences in approach. We need to ask, for example, why two Jews—Jesus and Paul—used such different terms: was it the result of their different upbringing, situation and experience? We have already seen one important and vital shift of perspective between them, caused by the resurrection. Inevitably, the teaching of Paul centres on Jesus himself, and on what God has done through him. His gospel is a gospel about Jesus Christ, and not the gospel which Jesus himself taught. But it seems to me to be possible to exaggerate the differences between them, by asking the wrong questions; by concentrating on questions about Christological titles, which tend to lead to negative results, or about Jesus' understanding of his own death, where the evidence is scanty. I suggest that we can trace a continuity between them in other—perhaps less obvious and impressive—ways. That there is a shift in interpretation and emphasis between Jesus and Paul is undeniable, and the shift is a Christological one. But I wonder whether it has not been a mistake to try to do what has so often been attempted—that is to try to trace the continuity between Jesus and Paul by showing a continuity in the understanding of the role of Jesus himself in the drama of salvation. The continuity which we do find is a common understanding of the relationship between God and man—expressed in different ways, yet basically similar; an understanding which led Jesus to the Cross—and which for Paul was focused in the Cross. The differences in vocabulary and imagery, orientation and situation, must not be allowed to obscure a continuity in theological stance. Of course there is diversity in the New Testament; but there is also continuity.

THREE

As in Adam, so in Christ

In the last chapter we looked at some of the summaries of
the gospel in Paul's letters, including the one with which he
opens his letter to the Romans: the gospel as Paul understands it is 'about the Son of God, who was descended from
David according to the flesh, and was proclaimed Son of
God in power according to the Spirit of holiness by the
resurrection from the dead'.[1] Reading on through the first
three chapters of Romans after the introductory paragraph, however, one might wonder whether Paul has forgotten about the gospel. He is apparently carried away by
his own description of mankind's wickedness and deprav-
ity: Jew and Gentile alike are proved to be unrighteous in
God's sight, and so come under condemnation. What
seems like a lengthy digression is, of course, necessary to
Paul's argument; he is concerned to demonstrate mankind's universal need for salvation. No one is righteous. His
picture in these opening chapters can be summed up as a
description of mankind 'in Adam'. Paul would not have felt
the necessity to undertake the task of demythologizing the
Old Testament. Yet what he is in effect doing here is to
demythologize Adam. He does not argue that because
Adam fell, all men are sinners—though this is what he *will*
argue at a later stage of his letter; rather, he begins by
demonstrating that all men *have* fallen. What he gives us
here is an account of what he later terms 'man in Adam'.

In Paul's understanding, mankind's basic sin is the
refusal to acknowledge God—to worship him and obey
him. Three times in chapter 1 he describes this basic sin;
man has forsaken the glory of God—that is refused to give
glory to God; he has exchanged the truth about God for a
lie; he has refused to acknowledge God. The sins which

[1] Romans 1:3 f.

36

Paul describes in the famous passage at the end of chapter 1 are the *result* of this condition, for those who sin are handed over by God to sinning. Those who cut themselves off from God are captured by an alien power. The sinful actions which Paul lists are not so much the crime in his view as the punishment for the crime; when man turns from God to sin, he is left by God to wallow in sin. The vocabulary which Paul uses in this section brings out clearly the link between man's sin and the sins into which this sin leads him. The process which he describes here was summed up neatly by W. S. Gilbert centuries later as an 'object all sublime . . . to let the punishment fit the crime'.

If this is mankind's universal condition, what remedy may be found? The Jewish answer was: in the Law. This had been the answer which Paul himself had once given, but it is one which he now totally rejects. The Law was unable to prevent man from sinning—on the contrary, it encourages sin, by suggesting various possibilities. And it has no remedy to offer for those who have sinned. Even if one claims to be blameless according to the Law (as Paul himself did), one is in fact guilty, because sin has such a grip on men and women that it is impossible for them to worship God and obey his commands from pure motives. Pious Jews may not wallow in the vices which Paul lists at the end of Romans 1; nevertheless they are unable to shake themselves free from that basic sin of mankind, which can be summed up as self-centredness, the concern with one's own well-being. The Law may be given by God himself, but it is incapable of saving anyone from himself.

Paul's analysis of the human condition is an acute one. We should probably all agree that it is well-nigh impossible to analyse one's own motives accurately. Is love ever genuinely altruistic? Can anyone avoid for very long thoughts about one's own well-being, happiness, security, reputation? Certainly the emphasis on reward in the Jewish religious system made it difficult to love God for his own sake. Nevertheless, Paul is surely being unfair to Judaism.

37

It is true that legalism will always be self-defeating—that man cannot, however hard he tries, justify himself in the eyes of God. Yet there is scope for forgiveness within the system of the Jewish Law; the Law is itself the gift of God and there is certainly room for grace to operate within the Law. Paul's antithesis between works and faith, Law and grace, has sometimes led commentators to suppose that Judaism knew nothing of faith and grace, and so to stress the break between the Old Testament and the New. Yet much of what Paul wrote can be paralleled by material in Jewish sources: Paul's emphasis on God's grace and man's sinfulness is certainly not new. Here, for example, are some lines taken from the Manual of Discipline, discovered at Qumran[2]:

'As for me, my justification is with God.
In his hand are the perfection of my way
    and the uprightness of my heart.
He will wipe out my transgression
    Through his righteousness . . .

'As for me, I belong to wicked mankind,
    to the company of ungodly flesh . . .
For mankind has no way,
    and man is unable to establish his steps
since justification is with God
    and perfection of way is out of His hand.

'As for me, if I stumble, the mercies of God
    shall be my eternal salvation.
If I stagger because of the sin of flesh,
    my justification shall be
    by the righteousness of God which endures for
        ever . . .

'He will draw me near by his grace
    and by his mercy will he bring my justification.

[2] 1QS xi and x, translation by G. Vermes, *The Dead Sea Scrolls in English* (Penguin)

He will judge me in the righteousness of his truth
    and in the greatness of his goodness
    He will pardon all my sins.

'Through his righteousness he will cleanse me
    of the uncleanness of man
    and of the sins of the children of men,
that I may confess to God his righteousness,
    and his majesty to the Most High.'

'I will declare his judgment concerning my sins,
and my transgressions shall be before my eyes as an
    engraved precept.
I will say to God 'My righteousness'
and 'Author of my goodness' to the Most High.'

Had I not revealed their source, you might perhaps have
thought that these passages were taken from some obscure
letter of St Paul! The ideas found here of universal sinfulness and of righteousness as something which belongs only
to God, of God's willingness to justify me, and of this action
of justification as almost equivalent to mercy—these are all
echoed in what Paul has to say. But there are two essential
differences. The first is that the author of the Qumran
document thinks of God's righteousness as something
which functions within the system of Law; it operates for
those who accept God's commands and obey them; God's
grace helps out, as it were, when members of the community who are living by this law fall short of all that God
requires. Paul, on the other hand, declares that God's
righteousness has been displayed *apart from* the Law[3]—an
idea which would surely have shocked the Qumran writer,
for the Law was almost by definition precisely the place
where God's righteousness was displayed. But Paul's point
is that it is by God's gracious activity, and not by man's
obedience to the Law, that man is saved. God's grace is
not confined to the Law—far from it; the locus of divine

[3] Romans 3:21

revelation has shifted—it is no longer centred on the Law but on Christ. As for the Law, this has in Paul's view been taken over by an alien power, i.e., Sin, in precisely the same way that man himself has been taken over.

In Paul's view, the Law—as a way of justifying oneself in the sight of God—is a failure. What was it that led him to the insight? What convinced him of the Law's inability to save man from sin? The traditional answer has been that it was Paul's own struggle with sin, immediately prior to his conversion, that led him to see the inadequacy of the Law; convinced of his own guilt because of his inability to fulfil the demands of the Law, he was gradually reduced to his knees, until he was set free from this tension by his conversion to Christianity. Paul himself does not describe his experience in these terms, however; on the contrary, he declares that he was blameless according to the Law.[4] The realization of his own guilt did not come, it seems, from any struggle to keep the Law before his conversion, but rather as a result of his conversion experience. We see Paul through the eyes of Augustine or Luther of Wesley when we see him as a man struggling—and failing—to keep the Law and so convicted of sin.

How, then, did Paul come to the conviction that the righteousness of God operates apart from the Law? It was, I suggest, part and parcel of his conversion to Christianity. The conviction that came to him that Jesus was Lord was a conviction that he had been raised from the dead; and this resurrection was itself a sign of divine approval—an act of vindication on God's part: it was by the resurrection, he says in Romans 1, that Christ was proclaimed Son of God—declared righteous. But Jesus had come under the condemnation of the Law, which announced that anyone who was hung on a tree was under a curse. The verdict of the Law was clearly wrong; the one whom the Law condemned had been declared righteous by God himself. The righteousness of God, vindicating one who was blameless

[4] Philippians 3:6

in his sight, has been demonstrated apart from the Law.

The second important difference between what the Qumran writer has to say and Paul's understanding of 'justification' is that the former understands the process entirely in terms of a future event. God *will* justify him, *will* pardon him. Paul, however, declares that the righteousness of God has already been manifested in the resurrection of Christ; and it is a righteousness which is already operative for Christian believers; they are already justified, already accepted. This, I think, is one of the essential differences between Paul and his Jewish predecessors. For him, the future hope has become a present reality; eschatology has been realized; future vindication has already taken place, in Christ.

Paul, then, rejects the Jewish solution to the problem of sin; as a means of salvation the Law does not work, and was never meant to work. A right relationship with God is offered to man freely, on the basis of the death and resurrection of Christ. But how does this work? How does the fact that one man was obedient to death and was proclaimed Lord by the resurrection make other men righteous in God's sight? Why should God justify those who have faith in Christ?

As so often happens, Paul is infuriatingly vague. He uses a variety of metaphors, and it would probably be wrong to seize on any one of them and assume that it is meant to be definitive. Certainly it would seem that his understanding of the atonement has been distorted by those who have forced particular interpretations into Paul's words. Paul rarely speaks of the death of Christ in terms of sacrifice, never interprets it in terms of punishment; later theologians developed their theories of the atonement and read them back into Paul's statements, but we must allow him to speak for himself.

But how does Paul think that the death and resurrection of Christ are related to the 'justification' of the believer? The idea of Christ's death as a sacrifice, which became

41

central in the thought of many later writers, occurs surprisingly rarely in Paul; we do find it used, however, in one well-known passage in Romans 3:21–31, where Paul moves from a description of human failure to an account of what 'justification' means. It is hardly surprising, after the description of the effects of sin in Romans chapters 1–3, that Christ's death is seen here as a means of expiation—a way of dealing with the sin which prevents reconciliation between God and man. The Greek term *hilastērion* which Paul uses here and which is best translated as 'expiation' was used also in the Greek Old Testament to refer to the cover of the 'ark' of the covenant, which was kept in the Holy of Holies, and which was 'cleansed' from the people's sins once a year by the High Priest with the blood of the sin-offering. It is possible that Paul has this ritual in mind in Romans 3, and that he is therefore thinking, not only of Christ's death as the means of getting rid of past sins, but of Christ himself as the place of reconciliation, where God and man are brought together. It was an obvious image for Paul to use, since the blood of the sin-offering was intended to remove the sins of those who had infringed the Law: far more effective than this remedy which the Law provides for minor offences, the death of Christ now achieved what the Law was incapable of doing, and made reconciliation between God and man possible.

Central to all that Paul has to say about justification is the notion that it is effected 'in Christ'—and this means, I believe, not simply that it comes about through Christ, through the agency of Christ, but that it depends upon the believer himself being 'in Christ'. We have been baptized into Christ, says Paul[5]—into his death and resurrection; what happens to him happens to us. We are crucified with him—but we are crucified with him in order that we may share his life[6], and this means that we share the verdict of 'not guilty' pronounced on him at the resurrection.

[5] Romans 6:3
[6] Galatians 2:20

42

Paul's understanding of this process presupposes a close identity of the believer with Christ. It is this idea which is summed up in his phrase 'in Christ'—a phrase with which many of us are now so familiar that we rarely stop to consider what it might mean; a phrase which is apparently without background and without parallel in the ancient world. There is nothing analogous—except the phrase with which Paul himself contrasts it, namely, the phrase 'in Adam'; Christ stands over against Adam as the new head of humanity. It seems that there are in Paul's view as it were two spheres; there is the sphere of humanity 'in Adam'—which includes everyone; and there is the sphere of those who are 'in Christ', who have been 'incorporated' into Christ; and if anyone is in Christ, says Paul, there is a new creation.[7] Those who have been baptized into Christ have shared in his death, and have been raised to life in a new existence. Now if one had died literally, physically, with Christ, or if Paul placed this change of existence at the moment of physical death, one might perhaps think of the two spheres as though they were two giant balloons, or as two space ships, linking up in space, and so enabling one to scramble from one sphere to the other. But in fact one can die with Christ and remain very much alive—and as long as one is alive, one remains in the physical sphere of life in Adam. The two spheres, then, must be seen not as touching at their edges, but as intersecting; Christians live in two spheres at once. But the reason why it is possible to move from one sphere to another—why those who are 'in Adam' can be baptized into Christ—the reason why these two spheres overlap at all is that Christ himself shared the condition of being 'in Adam'; the new humanity was created within the circle of the old.

Those who are 'in Christ' share in his resurrection life—and in order to do that they must first share in his death. But it is clear that there is in Paul's understanding a prior requirement; Christ must share our life and our

[7] 2 Corinthians 5:17

43

death, before we can share his; if we die with him out of one existence and are raised with him into a new existence, then it must be our life that he lives, and our death that he dies. He must be one with us, if we are to be one with him.

There are various passages in Paul's writings where he sums up neatly this idea of Christ sharing in what we are, in order that we might share what belongs to him. The neatest summary of all comes not from Paul himself but from Irenaeus: Christ became what we are, in order that we might become what he is.[8] This idea is expressed in different ways; in 2 Corinthians 8, for example, Paul reminds the Corinthians of 'the grace of our Lord Jesus Christ; though he was rich, yet for your sake he became poor, in order that by his poverty you might become rich.' The rich became poor, in order that the poor might become rich. But this is not a simple exchange, as though prince and pauper change places. In the fairy-story the prince is always finally unveiled, and receives back his riches; and so it is in the gospel: Christ shares our poverty—in order that we might share his riches. We have glanced already at Philippians 2, the famous passage which describes how Christ emptied himself and took the form of a slave; he was born in the likeness of men and was found in the fashion of men; finally he was obedient even to the point of death. Christ shared man's fate—and in the following chapter we learn how Christians share in his reward; picking up the vocabulary he has used in the earlier passage, Paul describes how we are to be fashioned after his likeness, and conformed to his glory. Christ shared in what we are, in order that we might share what he is.

There are other more forceful expressions of this idea. One of them comes in 2 Corinthians 5: Christ was made sin, writes Paul, in order that we might become the righteousness of God in him. Paul's thought here is so compressed that one needs to unpack it carefully. Clearly he is dealing

[8] *Against Heresies*, V preface

with the ideas with which we began this chapter—the problem of universal sinfulness and the need for a remedy; how can man be righteous in the eyes of God? Paul's answer is that Christ was made sin—was identified with the human condition of alienation from God, even to the extent of sharing the penalty for sin, which is death. But—and this is a stage in the argument which Paul does not bother to spell out here—Christ has been declared 'righteous' by his resurrection from the dead; because he was righteous, death had no power to hold him, and he has been acquitted. The result is that we become the righteousness of God in him—in other words, those who are 'in him', those who are joined to him, share in the resurrection and so share also in the righteousness which belongs to him. If Christ is righteous in God's sight, so are those who are in Christ, who die with him and rise with him. In the words of a hymn by Nicolaus zon Zinzendorf, translated by John Wesley:[9]

> 'Jesu, Thy blood and righteousness
> My beauty are, my glorious dress.'

Another forceful statement of this idea is found in Galatians 3:13, where Paul declares that Christ was made a curse for us, with the result that blessing has come even to the Gentiles. The fact that Christ came under the curse of the Law was demonstrated by his crucifixion, for according to Deuteronomy anyone who is hung on a tree is a curse to the land. But how upon earth can this curse bring about a blessing? The answer must be that it has been annulled; a power greater than that of the curse has not only wiped out the curse itself, but has converted it into blessing. The curse of the Law, which rests on those who do not keep its commands, has been annulled; blessing has overflowed, outside the boundary of the Law, to Gentiles. Once again, Paul presupposes the resurrection. It is in raising Christ from the dead that the curse of the Law is converted into

[9] *Methodist Hymn Book* 370

blessing and its restrictive power over man is destroyed.

In Philippians 2 and 2 Corinthians 5 and Galatians 3, Paul's thought is centred on the death of Christ. He was obedient to death—even the death of the Cross; in being made sin, he came under the power of death; the curse of the Law was demonstrated in the crucifixion. But when Paul speaks of Christ sharing in what we are, he has something wider than the death of Christ in mind; the Cross is not an isolated event. In 2 Corinthians 8, for example, we noticed that he speaks of Christ becoming poor, in order to make others rich. This wider perspective is seen, too, in Romans 8: 'What the Law could not do, God has done, sending his Son in the likeness of sinful flesh . . . so that the righeousness of the Law might be fulfilled in us . . . and all who are led by the Spirit of God are sons of God.' God sent his Son in our likeness . . . in order that we might become sons. What the *Law* could not do, *God* has done . . . in order that the righteousness of the Law might be fulfilled in us. How is this righteousness achieved in us?—this righteousness which the Law was unable to bring about? The intervening verses spell this out. If you are joined to Christ, says Paul to the Romans, you have both died because of sin, and been raised because of righteousness, i.e., you have shared the verdict and judgment passed on sin, and the acquittal and restoration pronounced on Christ; you have died with him and risen with him; the Spirit which inspires you to call God Father is the Spirit which raised Christ from the dead. We saw last time that Christ was declared to be Son of God according to the Spirit of holiness by the resurrection of the dead[10]; now we see that this same Spirit is responsible also for the declaration that *we* are sons of God. Our sonship depends on Christ's resurrection. It is at the resurrection that we become what he already is.

And just to make sure that we have understood Paul correctly, we can turn to Galatians 4:4 ff. and find a

[10] Romans 1:3 f.

similar passage. 'God sent forth his Son, born of woman, born under the Law, to redeem those who were under the Law, so that we cry "Abba! Father!".'

The idea which Paul explores in these various passages of Christ becoming what we are is one which I imagine most of us find comprehensible. It is true that Paul speaks of Christ being 'sent', and 'becoming', and some of us may regard this as the language of myth. But the idea which Paul is expressing here, of Christ's essential oneness with mankind is one which we can grasp well enough; Jesus is one with us in our humanity, and in our condition of alienation from God.

But how does this unity of Christ with mankind lead to our unity with him in a totally transformed situation? How can his death and life affect us? Why should we share in what he is and in what happens to him?

In thinking about the doctrine of the atonement, Christian theology has concentrated on the death of Jesus—and not surprisingly; this is clearly the heart of the matter. But if we stop there, and interpret atonement exclusively in terms of the Cross, we shall certainly misunderstand Paul. The death of Christ needs to be seen in connection with two other things. On the one hand, we have to focus also on the incarnation. This is clearly a dangerous term to use at the moment, and I do not want to be misunderstood. Moreover, it is not even a Pauline term. I use it not as a technical term, but simply as convenient shorthand, to sum up the idea which we have been exploring in this chapter—the idea of Christ's oneness with our humanity. It has been said again and again that Paul is not interested in the life of Jesus; he does not give us stories about the earthly Jesus. This is true enough, but I do not think that this means that Paul isolates the death of Jesus from his life: rather they belong to one pattern. It was because Christ was *born* under the Law that he came under the curse of the Law; it was because he was sent in the likeness of sinful flesh that he was made sin; clearest of all is the link made in

47

Philippians 2: Christ was born in the likeness of man, and was obedient to death, even the death of the Cross. The dying of Jesus is not to be separated from his previous living.

But neither is it to be separated from his resurrection life. And if the Cross of Christ must be linked with the idea of incarnation, it must certainly be linked also with the theme of resurrection. If Christ is not risen, your faith is vain, wrote Paul to the Corinthians.[11] Why? Because they are still in their sins—still in that state of sinfulness and alienation from God, still under the curse of the Law. Paul tells the Corinthians earlier that he preaches nothing except Christ crucified[12]—but it is clear that his preaching of the Cross includes preaching the resurrection. Christ died for us, so that we might live, Paul told the Thessalonians.[13] But he certainly did not mean that Christ and the Christian change places—that Christ is, as it were, a substitute, that he accepts punishment while others go free. Rather, it is a case always of sharing in Christ's condition. 'Christ died for us so that we might live *with him*'—and those final words are significant. Christ shares our life and death, and we are then able to share his death and resurrection.

As I understand what Paul is trying to say, he means that Christ shared in our humanity—and in all that this meant in terms of alienation from God and condemnation under the Law—right up to the point of death. But he was vindicated by God at the resurrection—pronounced righteous, acknowledged as God's Son. Those who are united to him, who share his death in baptism, share also his resurrection; and that means that they, too, are declared to be righteous by God, restored to the relationship of sonship to him. A new humanity has been created in Christ. There are, then, in Paul's view, two humanities. There is man in Adam, bound by the flesh, and enslaved to the sin which has

[11] 1 Corinthians 15:17
[12] 1 Corinthians 2:2
[13] 1 Thessalonians 5:10

invaded humanity; and there is man in Christ, raised to life by the power of the Spirit, declared righteous, i.e., 'justified' by God himself. The two humanities overlap in the life and death and resurrection of Jesus Christ.

If I have understood Paul correctly—and remembering all the ifs and buts of my initial chapter, I cannot claim to be certain that I have got him right—then there are obviously all sorts of problems as I try to relate what he is saying with my own experience in the twentieth century.

The first is this. Paul's notion of solidarity is foreign to us. It is true that one of the results of modern communications is that we are more aware of our links with people in remote countries—even if our neighbours are still strangers to us. We know perhaps what it is to feel a corporate responsibility when things go wrong—even though, very often, people seem to assume that when they blame society rather than individuals for the world's predicament, they are therefore absolved from guilt. I for one certainly feel myself more at home with Paul's idea of solidarity than with medieval notions of vicarious punishment. But I am still left asking: how does what happen to the one affect the many? How can I be reckoned as dead because Christ died? How can I be said to have been raised to life 'in him'? Words become familiar with use and we tend to think that we understand them; but what do they convey to someone who is not familiar with this kind of in-language? What do we mean when we say that what Adam did affected the whole of mankind? And what do we mean when we make similar statements about Christ?

You may well be thinking: we don't take this language about Adam literally; we don't interpret the Fall as an historical event any longer. We have demythologized Paul's language about man in Adam—along the lines which he himself seems to suggest—and interpreted it in terms of man in need of redemption. But what am I to do with the language about man 'in Christ', since Paul places these two phrases in parallel? Am I to demythologize this in the same way? Now to a certain extent, my answer to this question would be 'Yes'. One of the interesting things about Paul's Christology—and, indeed, about the Christology of New testament writers in general—is that many of the terms which are applied to Christ are terms which describe his humanity. If one explores the background of terms such as 'image of God', 'glory of God', 'Son of God'—even the term 'the Son of Man' in the gospels—one finds that they describe man as he is meant to be in God's purpose; Adam before the Fall, in an obedient relationship with God. In contrasting Adam and Christ, Paul is contrasting man as he is and man as he is meant to be.

But this is clearly to answer only half my problem; Adam and Christ may represent two contrasting humanities, two modes of life, but the two figures who represent them are an ill-balanced pair—the one mythical, the other historical. And here I come to my second problem—which is that the whole scheme of redemption, as Paul understands it, is set against an eschatological backcloth which made sense to him but no longer makes sense to me. His understanding of history moves from an original creation of a perfect world, through the Fall to everything which follows, i.e., the whole course of human history. What Jewish apocryphal writers longed for, and what Paul believed was taking place, was the restoration of the world to God's original purpose; in Christ, the process is reversed, man is recreated, the world brought back to order. So Paul points forward to the future glory. Creation itself, he writes in Romans[14], waits for the revelation of God's sons (i.e., Christians); for creation was subjected to futility—but soon it is to be set free from its bondage to decay. There is no need for me to spell out the difficulty of relating this picture to the world in which we live which shows no sign of being set free from bondage to decay. Do we demythologize this picture, also—or quietly forget it? And if we demythologize each end of Paul's understanding of salvation history, the Fall and the

[14] Romans 8:19 ff.

Restoration—what happens to the turning-point in the middle, which is focused on the figure of Christ?

These are immense problems, and they are problems to which we must return, since they are the questions which lie at the centre of the present theological debate. What I would like to say at this point is that if Paul's understanding of the death and resurrection of Christ are expressed in terms which belong to this eschatological framework, then we must recognize that his language makes sense within that framework, but cannot necessarily be translated very easily into our own thought-forms. We must remember that his understanding of God's action in Christ is expressed in imagery which belongs to a world-view which is very different from our own. What so often happens is that images are treated as though they had cash value in themselves. We shall not necessarily be able to give a one-for-one translation of Paul's ideas into our own terms.

Two final points. The first is that interpreters of Paul have often tended to understand what he has to say in a very individualistic way. It is natural for Christians to interpret his words in terms of their own experience—and of course they are right to do so. But I think we should remember that Paul himself was probably thinking in much more corporate terms; Paul's outlook was world-wide—his concern was with the salvation of mankind; it is later theology which became obsessed with the question of personal salvation.

The second is this. Later theology, as I have already said, tended to concentrate on the death of Christ in thinking about the atonement, and to exclude the resurrection. This was perhaps due to the use of sacrificial language, which was obviously appropriate—language which was used especially by the author to the Hebrews. But Paul is not only far more concerned with the resurrection than we sometimes remember—he is also far *less* concerned with sin. Contrary to popular opinion, Paul did not spend all this time talking about man's sin. True, he describes sin in the opening chapters of Romans; but then he tells his readers that sin belongs to their past life, and they have died to sin.[15] They have been raised to a new life—and they should get on with living it. Paul's attention is focused, not on sin, but on the righteousness which comes through Christ; on the life which works through death, and on the power which overcomes weakness. How he thinks this works is our subject in a later chapter.

[15] Romans 6:1 f.

FOUR

God was in Christ

In the first chapter I suggested that it is all too easy for us to read our own theological position back into the words of St Paul. We force his statements into line with our own categories, and assume that terms had the same meaning for him as for us. In addition to all the obvious barriers of differences in language, culture, time and custom, there is the significant divide caused by the formation of the canon. Hastily written letters came to be treated as holy scripture; Paul the interpreter became Paul the interpreted. Various ways of expressing belief became credal formulae; explorations in theological understanding became the basis of doctrinal statements.

This is especially true in the field of Christology, which is, of course, at the centre of theological thinking in the New Testament. Christological terms have become for us terms which are full of meaning—having a life and existence of their own. We assume that they already had that content in first-century Judaism; that they were ready-made concepts, and that all that had to be done was to identify Jesus with figures existing already in a clearly defined messianic scheme. We tend to treat a statement such as 'Jesus is the Christ' rather as though it were an algebraic formula in which we discover that x is equivalent to y; as though it offered a precise definition of who and what Jesus was.

Unfortunately the problem is much more complicated than this. We, of course, think we know what the term 'Christ/Messiah' means, because we have built up a composite picture of Messiahship. But our picture is based largely on certain Old Testament texts which were not originally about a Messiah at all, but have been interpreted messianically in the light of Christian experience. The popular understanding of what was expected of the Messiah rests to a large extent on the libretto of Handel's oratorio. Unfortunately we do not know what the first-century man in the streets of Jerusalem expected of a Messiah at all; a Gallup poll might have revealed a great variety of hopes—and they would have been influenced considerably by the prevailing political situation. In view of the Roman occupation, the prevailing hope would undoubtedly have been for some kind of political figure, a true son of David who would lead his people to victory. But strictly speaking it is false to speak of *the* Jewish hope for the Messiah; the Old Testament references are to *an* anointed one. The pre-Christian hope is much more nebulous, much more elastic, than we tend to assume. Interestingly enough, it is not so much in this case that the Christian idea of the Messiah has been imposed upon the Jewish hope; rather, because the Jews did not accept Jesus as their Messiah, New Testament scholars have pieced together a picture of a Jewish ideal figure—a picture which, it is suggested, Jesus rejected. Whether or not belief in such a figure was an important factor in the situation, however, we do not know. It is in this kind of area—how the ordinary first-century Jew felt and what he believed and hoped—that our evidence is so sadly scanty.

The way in which we speak of Jesus as the Messiah—with a capital M—demonstrates the way in which we tend to give these terms some kind of objective reality. But, as I suggested earlier, the term has meaning only within a particular culture. Unless I belong to that culture, to say that Jesus is the Messiah has no significance. So, too, with that strange term 'the Son of man'. A well-known American New Testament scholar, John Knox, who finds it impossible to believe that Jesus thought of himself as the Son of man, tells of a colleague who protested, 'But suppose he *was* the Son of man?' John Knox comments, 'Now I find such a question very hard to deal with, not because of what it asks for, but because of what it seems to presuppose. It seems to ascribe to the 'Son of man' objective and personal reality. It seems to assume that there was, and is, a Son of man. But what does the phrase 'Son of man' . . . really designate? Must we not say that it stands for an idea, or an image, in the minds of certain ancient Jews? One can trace to some extent the beginning and development of this idea or image in Jewish culture. But do we for a moment suppose that it is the name of any actual person—that the Son of man in fact exists or ever existed?'[1] Our problem arises, I suspect, because terms which were used to express the *role* of Jesus (and which did so in a meaningful and forceful way when they were first used) quickly became treated as *titles* when they were detached from their original context. To say that Jesus is God's anointed is to say something about his role and function; and when Jesus spoke of himself as the Son of man (as I believe he did) then he was saying something about his understanding of his own position in God's plan and purpose—he was describing his role and function, not claiming a title. It is when we treat these statements as declarations about Jesus' *identity* that we misunderstand them. It is precisely because I think that John Knox is *right* to interpret 'the Son of man' as an image rather than a title, that I think he is *wrong* to argue that Jesus could not have used it of himself.

What, then, of the term 'Son of God'? Is this used of Jesus as a title? One of the worrying things about the 'debate' which followed the publication of *The Myth of God Incarnate* was the way in which some of those who were anxious to defend the faith appealed to the occurrence of the phrase 'Son of God' in the New Testament—as though it were used there with all the significance which it has in the later creeds: they assumed that this was enough to prove the 'divinity' of Christ. Perhaps, then, there is still need to remind ourselves of the precise ways in which the term *is* used.

In Romans 1:3 f., Paul introduces himself to the Roman Christians and begins his letter—which is in effect a

[1] John Knox, *The Death of Christ* (Collins 1959), pp.71 f.

statement of his theological position—with a summary of the gospel which many scholars think is a quotation of a mini-creed. The gospel is 'about God's Son, who was descended from David according to the flesh, and designated Son of God in power according to the Spirit of holiness by the resurrection from the dead? One reason for this belief that Paul is quoting is that what he writes here does not fit exactly into the pattern which scholars think appropriate for Paul: it includes a disproportionately large amount of unusual vocabulary, and theological statements which are untypical of Paul's position. After my gloomy assessment of the accuracy of our knowledge of Paul himself, you will realize that I am dubious as to whether or not we have sufficient evidence on which to make this kind of judgment! But if these scholars are right, then it means that at a very early date, and so at an early stage in Christian theological development, we have what may be an example of a credal statement being quoted and adapted; quoted because it expressed—however inadequately—Christian belief; adapted in order to express more clearly what Paul felt to be important; quoted because it was part of the tradition which had been handed down; but adapted because it was already wearing thin as Christianity moved across the boundaries of language and culture and environment, and needed to be re-expressed in ways appropriate to its setting. It seems that our problem of cultural relativity may not be such a modern problem after all!

And already, as part of this mini-creed (if that is what it is), we have the confession that Jesus is Son of God. The way in which we interpret this statement will depend to a large extent on the background from which we assume it to have been drawn.

It is often assumed that the phrase 'Son of God' was a Jewish messianic title. This is perhaps due to the evangelists, who tend to use it as an equivalent for 'Messiah'. It may be that what they are doing is to 'translate' a Jewish term into what seemed an equivalent Greek one for the benefit of Hellenistic Christians. We need to ask, therefore, whether it has a background within Judaism, and whether it would have been an appropriate term for Jews to use of one whom they thought of as God's anointed one.

There is in fact no evidence that the phrase was ever used in pre-Christian Judaism as a messianic title. It is true that in a couple of passages in the Old Testament the king is *addressed* as God's Son. In Psalm 2:7 we read 'The Lord said to me, "You are my son, today I have begotten you" '. And in 2 Samuel 7:14 we have the promise of God to David concerning David's son: 'I will be his father, and he will be my son.' Presumably if the present king is referred to in this way, a future, messianic king could also be spoken of as God's Son. But notice that we do not have a title here; rather we have a description of a relationship.

There is a singular lack of evidence in the Old Testament, then, for the phrase 'Son of God' being used as any kind of title. The extra-biblical evidence adds very little to the picture. It is true that a couple of fragments from Qumran have come to light recently and caused much excitement, but only one of them is significant. In the first[2], the passage from 2 Samuel 7, 'You are my son', is interpreted as referring to 'the sprout of David'. This is a perfectly straightforward piece of biblical exegesis, and certainly does not indicate that the term 'Son' was ever used as a title. In the second[3], there are only a few words preserved, and the gaps make interpretation difficult; but one vital line is clear, and this contains the words: 'You shall be called the son of God, and son of the Most High.' But who is being addressed? What is left gives no clue—though the most likely guess would seem to be that the words are being spoken to a future Jewish king, i.e., a messianic figure. If so, then here we do have the use of the term 'Son of God' as a title; but notice that it is in the vocative—it is really only an application of that passage in 2 Samuel 7. We are still a long way

[2] 4Q Florilegium
[3] 4Q ps Dan A[a]

from using the phrase 'the Son of God' as a title for Messiah.

So the Jewish evidence suggests that it might well seem *appropriate* to describe a messianic figure (or at least address him) as 'Son of God'. But that is very different from saying that 'Son of God' would necessarily be interpreted by Jewish readers as meaning 'Messiah', or that the two were in any sense equivalent terms.

In fact, the term 'Son of God' has a much wider use in Jewish literature. In the Old Testament it is primarily Israel who is spoken of as God's son, and the idea of sonship expresses both preciousness and privilege. The image of God's fatherhood and the people's sonship expresses two sides of the covenant relationship—namely election and obedience; or perhaps it would be more accurate to say 'disobedience', since most of the Old Testament passages complain about Israel's unworthy behaviour. Later Jewish literature was more optimistic, and referred to the hope for the future, when Israel would be restored to a proper relationship of obedience. It was natural enough that the image should be narrowed down to the righteous within the community, and so came to be used of the righteous man in particular, as in the famous passages in Wisdom 2 and 5[4]: if the righteous man is God's son, he will help him and deliver him; at the judgment, the righteous man is numbered among the sons of God.

The image of sonship, then, is used for describing the relationship between God and his chosen people; it symbolizes the ideas of election and obedience. It is not really a title; rather it describes a role.

The absence of the title 'Son of God' in Judaism has led many scholars to look to Hellenism for the background of New Testament usage. It has been suggested that it first came into use for Jesus in Gentile Christian circles, influenced by the Hellenistic notion of the 'divine man', a figure who was known to possess supernatural power because of

[4] Wisdom 2:12–20; 5:1–5

his ability to work miracles. Evidence for this notion, too, is scanty. It has been well said that there are far more references to the figure of the 'divine man' in the pages of modern scholarship than in all the pages of antiquity! If this were the background of the New Testament references to Jesus as Son of God, then we would expect to find the term used especially in relation to the idea of divine power; for example, in the gospels we would expect to find it used in miracle stories. Is this how Paul uses the term? It seems worth looking at the passages where the term actually occurs in the Pauline writings, and enquiring into its function.

We have seen already that Paul uses the term in the opening lines of Romans. In fact he uses it twice: the gospel is about God's Son . . . who was declared Son of God by the resurrection of the dead. But side by side with this statement that he was declared Son of God according to the Spirit, we have the parallel statement that he was Son of David according to the flesh. The passage bristles with theological problems, and I do not want to get embroiled in them. What I want to point out is that Paul first tells us that the gospel is about God's Son; and that he then says that he (i.e., God's Son) was . . . (the meaning of the verb is disputed) by the resurrection of the dead. Since Paul sees no contradiction between these two statements, it seems that we must translate my missing verb as 'declared/ proclaimed' rather than as 'made/appointed'. It was at the resurrection that Jesus' sonship was made known. This link between resurrection and sonship is illuminating, since the resurrection is also the vindication of Christ, the declaration of his righteousness in the eyes of God.

A little further on in this chapter, in verse 9, Paul refers again to the gospel about God's Son. So twice over in these introductory verses Paul makes sure that his readers know that the source of the gospel is God, and that the content of the gospel is God's Son.

We need to move on to 5:10 for another reference to the

Son of God, and here we have another succinct statement of the gospel: 'If while we were enemies we were reconciled to God through the death of his Son, how much more, being reconciled, shall we be saved by his life.' This statement occurs at a crucial point in the argument of Romans, where Paul sums up his understanding of the way in which God redeems mankind in Christ. His theme is paradoxical: our reconciliation to God is achieved by the death of his Son. Paul appeals to this foundation stone of the gospel, in order to argue that we have nothing to fear: if we have been reconciled to God by Christ's death, we shall be saved from future wrath. Why does Paul use the term 'Son' at this point? Is it accidental? Is it simply a variation? Or is it perhaps in order to emphasize the unity of purpose between God and his Son? The death of Christ demonstrates not God's displeasure but the Son's obedience: reconciliation between God and man is brought about, not by unilateral action on God's part, but by an action in which Father and Son were at one, and in which at-one-ment between God and man were therefore focused. The unity of purpose between God and his Son becomes, as it were, the nucleus of the sphere of reconciliation between God and man. Paul is appealing here to the loving purpose of God, which is achieved through the obedience of his Son Jesus. As he said in his opening verses, the gospel is founded in the purpose of God, and it is about God's Son. This passage expresses Paul's confidence in the loving activity of God; it has been demonstrated in the past in his Son, and will be continued in the future.

The remaining references to 'Son of God' in Romans all occur in chapter 8. In verse 3 we have a famous summary of the gospel: 'What the Law could not do, God has done . . . sending his own Son in the likeness of sin and flesh.' Once again, Paul's theme here is the loving purpose of God, achieved this time through the sending of his Son: what the *Law* could not do, because of the weakness of flesh, and the disobedience of mankind, *God* has done through the obedience of his Son. But for the end of the matter we need to move on to verse 29: the result of God's purpose, achieved through the sending of his Son, is that we are conformed to the likeness of his Son, who is the first-born among many brothers.

One of the problems of trying to expound St Paul in the 1970s is that he seems to us to be guilty of using sexist language; he almost invariably uses masculines; it certainly would not have occurred to him to try to concoct the Greek equivalent of a modern monstrosity such as 'chairperson'. It is an interesting example of the effect which our environment has on our understanding of language that Paul's references to 'brothers' or 'sons' strike us now in a way which they did not before Women's Lib. trained our eyes and ears to notice these niceties. It is difficult to know how to deal with this problem. We could perhaps translate 'sons' as 'children'—but if we do we lose the verbal link that Paul makes between God's only Son and those who become his 'sons'. We could perhaps speak of 'sons and daughters'; but in Paul's world it was the son, not the daughter, who enjoyed all the privileges, and Paul's point is precisely that *all* Christians enjoy these privileges, whatever their sex or race or status. Perhaps I at least may opt to use Paul's terms 'sons' and 'brothers' without being accused of sexist bias! It is clear that in this present passage, at any rate, the masculine embraces the feminine.

The point which seems to me to be vital in trying to understand Romans 8 is the link between verse 3 and verse 29. The two statements, taken together, express one of Paul's central themes: God sent his Son . . . in *our* condition . . . in order that we might share *his*—that is, so that we might become sons of God. The close connection between these two statements is brought out in the argument of the intervening verses, where Paul summarizes his understanding of redemption. The Son of God shares our human condition; by his death he dies to sin and condemns sin; those who—in turn—are content to share his death (by baptism) share also in his resurrection. Paul underlines the parallel here between Christ's experience and ours—but notice also the significant difference. It is through death that we come to life; it is through humiliation that we come to glory; we are crucified with him, in order that we may be raised with him. In other words, the Christian shares in the experience of Christ. And yet there is a crucial difference; through this process, says Paul, we become sons of God; but Christ does not become Son of God—he *is* Son of God. We do not share with him in a process of becoming sons of God—rather we share in what Christ already is. God sends one who is his Son—and we become sons of God. For us, resurrection with Christ is a transformation; but we are transformed to become what Christ already is. It seems that for Paul the resurrection of Christ is much more a vindication, an acknowledgment of the truth, an entering into an inheritance; he is declared Son of God by the resurrection. Paul is spelling out here precisely the same ideas as he summarized in Romans 1:3 f. The gospel is about God's Son—who in human terms is son of David, but is declared Son of God (which he already is) by the resurrection.

The final reference to 'Son of God' comes in Romans 8:32. 'He who did not spare his own Son' but gave him up for us all, how will he not also give us all things with him?' God is on our side, and therefore we need have no fears for the future. Paul's argument here is exactly parallel to the one he used in 5:10: God has acted in a certain way in the past; we may therefore be confident about the future. And the basic fact which gives us confidence is the same: God gave his Son up for us, that is he has reconciled us to himself *in his Son*. Salvation has taken place in Jesus—this is why the future is guaranteed.

In Romans, then, we find Paul using the term 'Son of God' in the opening paragraph, when he is introducing his Gospel as being about God's Son. And in the later chapters, we find him referring back to this understanding of the Gospel. He uses the term in passages where he speaks about God's saving act in Christ, and I suggest that he uses it in order to underline the fact that God's purpose of salvation is brought about through one who (being Son) acts in accordance with and in obedience to that purpose; what happens in Christ, therefore, is the activity of God himself.

One swallow does not make a summer, and one epistle is hardly a fair sample of Paul's thought. But a similar pattern emerges in Galatians. Once again, we find a basic reference to the gospel in the first chapter. In 1:16, Paul describes his own conversion as the time when it pleased God 'to reveal his Son in me'. Commentators have often been puzzled by this phrase 'in me', and translators have not known what to do with it—they have mostly translated it as '*to* me'. But Paul is not, I am sure, meaning that he received a divine revelation of the content of the Gospel; he means more than the fact that he came to believe that Jesus was Son of God. 'God revealed his Son in me'. He means, I think, that from this point on, his life was taken over by a new power. The gospel became his way of living—and that means that the pattern of the gospel—of life through death, glory through humility, strength through weakness—was stamped upon him. The image of Christ's life—and death—was now seen in his. Once again, then, Paul is referring to his basic understanding of the gospel—and it is a gospel, so he stresses here, which has its origin with God, not men; it is God, not men, to whom he owes his call to be an apostle; it is God who gave him the gospel; and the gospel is about God's Son.

In the following chapter, we find a famous summary of the Christian life; Paul's life, he tells us, is lived 'by faith in the Son of God, who loved me and gave himself for me'. In this passage, as in Romans 5:10 and 8:32, Paul is expressing his confidence in God. Life for Paul means reliance upon the fact that the Son of God has loved him and given himself for him. The verb 'he gave himself' used here is the same as that which is used in Romans 8 for 'God gave his Son'. What was described in Romans as the loving purpose

63

of God—in giving up his Son—is here described as the action of the Son of God—he loved me and gave himself up for me. But this is not a great step; it simply draws out what is already implied in Paul's language about the 'Son'. The Son is one who is obedient to his Father's will and shares his Father's purposes. Since the Son of God is here the subject of the verb, it is not surprising that Paul speaks here of '*the* Son of God', rather than of 'God's Son' or 'his Son' as he normally does elsewhere.

Finally in Galatians, we find Paul telling us in chapter 4 that 'God sent his Son, born of woman, born under the Law . . .' and that 'God has sent the Spirit of his Son into our hearts . . .' The theme of this passage is remarkably close to that in Romans 8. Here as there, Paul speaks of God sending his Son, who shares our condition in order that *we* might receive adoption and become sons of God. This is authenticated by God sending the Spirit of his Son into our hearts; we cry 'Abba', using the same word as was used by Jesus. We share his Sonship, his relationship to God. Once again, Paul is here summing up his understanding of the meaning of redemption; this is what God has done—and this is why there is no need for men to chase after righteousness or try to keep the Law or accept circumcision. The loving purpose of God was achieved through his Son, whom he sent, and who shared in his purposes.

And so we could go on—looking at the uses of the term 'Son of God' in 1 and 2 Corinthians, in 1 Thessalonians, in Colossians.[5] But perhaps we have looked at enough

[5] 1 Corinthians 1:9 sums up our confidence in God, who has called us into the fellowship of his Son; central to 1 Corinthians 15:28 is the theme of the Son's obedience to the Father. 2 Corinthians 1:19 appeals to the fact that the character and purposes of God are expressed in the Son. 1 Thessalonians 1:10 also expresses confidence in God; we wait for the appearance of his Son from heaven, and he will save us from wrath. In Colossians 1:13, we are reminded that God has transferred us from the power of darkness and placed us in the kingdom of his Son. It is perhaps significant that the author of Ephesians (who is probably not Paul) uses the term in a different kind ot context altogether in Ephesians 4:13.

evidence for me to suggest that the term is not used in either Romans or Galatians in a haphazard way—that it is not simply one title for Christ which is interchangeable with any other title. It still has a functional use—it is used by Paul in particular contexts to express certain ideas. On the one hand, it expresses the idea that this is the one *through* whom God has chosen to work in bringing about his redemptive purposes; on the other, that this is the one who is fully obedient to God and who was willing to be used as his instrument. The two ideas are, of course, two sides of one coin; and there is an obvious parallel with the use of the term in Jewish literature. It looks as if Judaism, rather than Hellenistic religion, is the background for Paul's use of the term.

If we are to understand Paul, then it is essential that we forget our presuppositions. Just how difficult it is to do this seems to me to be admirably demonstrated when we think about this particular term. To us, for example, it inevitably conveys the idea of pre-existence—and so we assume that this was true for Paul also. Here is one New Testament scholar arguing that this is so: 'In one group of passages,' he writes, ' "Son of God" contains the ideas of the pre-existence, career and destiny of the revealer.' In support he quotes Philippians 2:6 ff.—but has to admit that the term 'Son of God' does not actually occur in that passage![6] We must not read our ideas into Paul and assume that he shared the ideas which belong to later periods and different cultures. Nor must we read Paul through Greek spectacles if he is in fact writing in Jewish terms.

But you may well say to me that there are a couple of passages in which Paul speaks of God 'sending his Son'; surely these imply the notion of pre-existence? Logically, the answer must of course be 'yes'—and I suspect that we have here the beginning of the idea. But this is very

[6] H. Conzelmann, *An Outline of the Theology of the New Testament* (Eng. Tr. SCM 1969), pp.78 f.

65

different from saying that the term 'Son of God' in itself implies and necessitates the idea of pre-existence; that is not, I think, the thought which concerns Paul even in these passages; when he says that God sent his Son, his concern is with what *God has done*, rather than with what *Jesus is*. In other words, the question which he is concerned to answer was very different from the one which confronted later theologians when they enquired about the pre-existence of Christ.

What conclusions can we draw from this study of Paul's use of the term 'Son of God'?

First, I think it should serve as a warning to us not to appeal too easily to statements in the New Testament, as though there were a straightforward one-to-one relationship between their language and ours. Paul does not, it seems to me, use the term in order to express 'the divinity' of Christ. It is true that Christ's sonship is unique; in this respect there is an important difference between Paul's use of the term and that found in the Old Testament. But the idea of his sonship is one which unites him with men and women, as well as with God. On the one hand, the term expresses what Paul sums up neatly elsewhere when he declares 'God was in Christ'; what God is and what he does are both revealed in his Son, for the Son reproduces his father's character and purpose. On the other hand, the idea of Christ's sonship expresses also what man is meant to be. As son of God Israel should have been obedient to God; this obedience has now been fulfilled, so Paul argues, in the person of Jesus Christ. But it is something in which all Christians are called to share.

Secondly, we must beware of judging the 'orthodoxy' of New Testament Christological statements by the standards of a later period. 'Son of God' is one example of several Christological terms which are used in the New Testament in a very different way from that which became common at a later date. It is interesting that terms which to us seem to represent what we might well describe as a 'high' Christology were apparently used in the New Testament period to express the true humanity of Christ. He is, for example, 'the image of God'[7]: the suggestion that the background of this phrase is to be found in Genesis 1 is confirmed by the fact that we are told that we are taking on the same image, and are urged to put on the new man existing in Christ. The idea of Christ as God's 'glory'[8] would seem to have the same background, and it may well be that the statement that Christ was 'in the form of God'[9] is another deliberate comparison and contrast with Adam. Similar ideas seem to lie behind the term 'the Son of man' in the gospels and the language used of Christ in Hebrews 1. But the fact that these terms are about the 'humanity' of Christ does not mean that they do *not*, in fact, represent a 'high' Christology. If we suppose that it is only statements about the 'divinity' of Christ—about his metaphysical being—which offer us a 'high' Christology, then we are certainly viewing the New Testament through Chalcedonian spectacles.

Thirdly, although Paul uses the term 'Son of God' as a title, we have argued that it occurs in contexts where it is especially appropriate; in other words, it expresses a particular role. It is perhaps significant that the most common form of the phrase in Paul's letters is 'his Son' (occasionally written in full as 'God's Son') rather than '*the* Son of God'; the stress is on Christ's relationship to God, and on his obedience to God's purpose and plan. Paul's Christology is functional, in the sense that he is primarily concerned to express what Christ does, and what God does through him, not his metaphysical being. It is arguable that by concentrating on the problem of Christological titles in the New Testament, biblical scholars have changed terms which originally conveyed this idea of function into titles which have a life of their own.[10] Yet it seems that for Paul the real

[7] Colossians 1:15
[8] 2 Corinthians 3:7–4:6
[9] Philippians 2:6

67

point is not that A is identified with B ('Jesus is the Son of God') but that A is discovered to have the characteristics of B (Jesus is demonstrated to be God's Son, both by God's activity and his own). Once again, because we view the material from a later perspective, we ask different questions and so distort Paul's meaning when we try to force our answers onto his material.

[10] A good example of this is seen in the way in which New Testament scholars have been concerned to answer the question 'Did the New Testament writers identify Jesus with the Suffering Servant?' Yet the term 'Suffering Servant' never occurs in the New Testament, and even the term 'Servant' is used only rarely, in the early chapters of Acts; moreover, we have no evidence that 'the Servant' was ever used as a title in contemporary Judaism. The proper question to ask in this case is whether Jesus is understood to be exercising the role which is described in Isaiah 53—not whether he is 'identified' with some imaginary figure.

FIVE

Have This Mind in You

We looked earlier at one of the most characteristic phrases in Paul's writings—the phrase 'in Christ'. He uses it frequently, and yet it remains enigmatic—an odd phrase without any real parallel. Sometimes it seems to have the meaning 'by Christ' or 'through Christ', and one might perhaps translate it in that way; at other times one feels that it might be suitably translated as 'Christian'. Sometimes the force of the 'in' seems to be almost literal—the preposition, that is, has a local sense; the believer is *in* Christ, joined to him. This seems to be the idea which lies behind the passages we looked at which speak about the believer's redemption in Christ. The phrase expresses the identification of the believer with Christ, which follows Christ's identification with mankind. I suggested that this might be one way of understanding what Paul means by 'justification'. Christ is vindicated by God at the resurrection—pronounced innocent of the charges brought against him under the Law, acquitted by God himself and pronounced righteous. Those who identify themselves with his death to sin are identified also with his resurrection—they are 'in him', and share in his acquittal. Just as all men share in what happened to Adam because they are in Adam, so those who are in Christ share in what happened to him. By his failure to give glory to God, Adam became a distortion of what man was meant to be. But Christ is the very reverse—he is man as he is meant to be, living as he was meant to live; he is the 'proper man' as Luther put it. Those who are 'in Christ' are no longer living in the state of alienation from God described by Paul in the early chapters of Romans, no longer bogged down by sin, and no longer under condemnation. Paul sums up the consequence in Romans 8:1: 'There is therefore now no condemnation for those who

69

are in Christ Jesus.' We share his status—that of sons—and are brought into a right relationship with God. This is what Paul means by 'justification'; it is a being put right with God. Righteousness is never something which believers possess—it is never their own. It is something which belongs to Christ—and those who are in him share it. It is 'in Christ' that God and man are reconciled. Christ is the place where salvation is found.

But this justification—the being brought into a right relationship with God—is only the beginning. 'He died for us, so that we might live with him', writes Paul to the Thessalonians—and this 'living' is an on-going process. It is especially in thinking about the consequences of our being raised with Christ that Paul uses the phrase 'in Christ'. What does it mean to share the resurrection life of Christ—to live in him?

This idea of living in Christ has sometimes been described as Pauline mysticism. It is not a good term, for Paul is certainly not describing what is normally understood by mysticism. What he is describing is better understood on the analogy of a very close relationship between two people—so close that they interpenetrate one another at every level. The phrase 'in Christ' may be an odd one, and if we think of men and women in very individualistic terms, each a complete entity in himself or herself, we shall certainly not understand what Paul is trying to convey. But we know that we are not like that; we are linked to one another in a great variety of ways—sometimes at a superficial level, but often in a much deeper way; two people can grow together and become one entity, their personalities locked together. So it is with the believer and Christ. Occasionally Paul expresses this in an intensely personal way—most of all in the famous passage in Galatians[1]: 'I have been crucified with Christ; nevertheless I live; yet it is no longer I, but Christ who lives in me. For the life which I now live in the flesh I live by faith—faith in the Son of God,

[1] Galatians 2:20

70

who loved me and gave himself for me.' But Paul does not often write in this intensely personal, individualistic way. Usually he seems to be describing the life of the community. When *he* writes about those who are 'in Christ' *we* should probably have written about the Church. We have already described being in Christ in terms of a sphere. We might perhaps try another geometric analogy, and think of this experience in terms of a graph; for being in Christ involves not only a vertical dimension—a relationship with him—but a horizontal dimension as well—the relationship with our fellow Christians, who are also in Christ; they, too, are in this sphere. As John Wesley put it, there is no such thing as a solitary Christian. To be in Christ is to be in the Church—that is in the universal Church. Discussions about church union might have progressed a great deal faster if only Christians had been more ready to recognize that their fellow Christians were already within this community, and that being a member of Christ is much more important than being a member of any *particular* Christian community. To separate oneself from other Christians is to put up barriers *within* Christ, to tear Christ apart—or, to use Paul's own forceful image, to dismember Christ. To be in Christ means for Paul inevitably (however much one may dislike it) being in the Church, joined to everyone else who is in Christ.

One way in which Paul described this dual relationship of the believer to Christ and to his fellow Christians was in the image of the body of Christ. This particular image has played an important role in the thought of some twentieth-century theologians—and I suspect that too much has been made of it. Paul would, I think, have been surprised to find that this image has been treated as though it represented a metaphysical reality; far from being this, one can almost see Paul trying the idea out, exploring its possibilities. And it is in many ways a very good image, for it expresses very well not only the relation of every believer to Christ, but the relation of each believer to every other believer. The whole

71

community is closely bound together. 'You are Christ's body', Paul tells the Corinthians, 'and each of you is a limb or organ of it'.

We are well accustomed to hearing modern ecumenical appeals based on Paul's image of the body; it is used repeatedly in arguments for unity. But Paul is in fact arguing in the opposite direction—he is arguing for diversity. The unity of the community is basic, and is assumed; it is true, of course, that Paul is arguing against those whose behaviour is leading towards fragmentation, towards the break-up of the community; but this is precisely because they are ignoring this basic unity. Paul argues for diversity, and for a sharing between the members of the one community of the variety of gifts which God has given. These gifts are intended for the community, and belong to the whole group. If one is going to grade the gifts, then the best are those which do most towards building up the community. If individuals glory in the gifts which have come to them, and forget that they are intended for the benefit of the community as a whole, this will lead to the break-up of that community instead of its strengthening. So we have Paul's famous description of the body, and the various parts which all have a part to play within it.

These various gifts, whatever they are, are all dependent on being in Christ. But Christian living is not simply a question of receiving spiritual gifts. The whole outlook of the Christian is determined by his new status in Christ. And here we come to what we may call the ethical consequences of life in Christ. For the Jew, the implications of his relationship with God were spelt out in the Law; those who were members of the covenant people accepted the obligation to keep the Law. Paul has demonstrated that the Law cannot bring us to a right relationship with God; this is to be found only by being in Christ. He has shown also that the covenant pointed forward to a faith-relationship with Christ. But this means that Christ has replaced the Law, not only as the way by which one is received as righteous by

God, but as the pattern of our obedience to God. The command of the Law was: 'Be holy—by separating yourselves from other nations outside the promises and the covenant; by keeping the commands of the Law; by circumcision; by keeping the festivals; by atoning sacrifices and rituals which deal with minor infringements.' But Paul is saying: 'Be holy, simply by being in Christ. Demonstrate that you belong to God by your Christ-like character.' So we find that when Paul uses the phrase 'in Christ' it is often to refer to the behaviour which ought to characterize the Christian—as, for example, in the command: 'As you received Christ Jesus as Lord, so live in him.'[2] It has been said that Paul's ethical teaching consists in saying 'Be what you are—in Christ'. Be what you are; you are in Christ, and that means being in a right relationship with God—which is impossible if you do not behave in a way which is compatible with God's own character. You are in Christ, and that means sharing the qualities which belong to Christ—goodness, holiness, wisdom, love, joy; then behave like it! Paul's basic ethical principal is very simple—almost too simple. Certainly one gathers from his letters that the members of his churches found this simple guideline much too difficult to put into practice! It is all very well for Paul to say 'Live in Christ' and 'Be like Christ'—but what does he mean? What does this involve, in terms of everyday, practical living? There seems to be a basic human instinct which likes to be told precisely what is required of one—even if one then protests about having to do it! It is much easier to keep a set of rules—or at least to try to—than to say in every situation: what is the Christ-like thing to do now? Certainly some of Paul's congregations hankered after a set of rules. Imagine yourself a member of one of those Galatian churches, in some obscure corner of Asia Minor. Paul has rushed through on a lightning evangelical campaign, has preached the gospel with tremendous verve, converted a small group of Jews and pagans to the new faith, and rushed off again.

[2] Colossians 2:6

What do you do next? No doubt you meet together to worship, and to think through your new faith. The only scriptures you have are those which we now call the Old Testament—scriptures which Paul had used and argued from in the course of his preaching, and which he constantly appealed to in the course of the letter which he will later write to the congregation. Your only guidance in reading these scriptures—apart from your own Christian experience—will be the things which you remember Paul to have said about them—in terms of their being fulfilled in Christ—and what the Jewish members of the congregation will be able to tell you about them, from their background of Jewish life and practice. It is small wonder if, as you study these documents, you come to the conclusion that your Christian faith implies that you ought to accept the obligations of the Law, as set out there, and to accept circumcision, the sign of the promise which was made to Abraham, and which was fulfilled in Christ. It is small wonder if you find it impossible to make the distinction which to Paul seemed so obvious, between the Law as pointing forwards to Christ and being a witness to him, and the Law as a code of ethics. How else should one work out this idea which Paul kept on about—that of 'living in Christ'—than by obeying the rules set out in the scriptures which one used as the basis of one's worship, and as the evidence for one's Christian faith?

There was, of course, an alternative. This was to disregard the teaching of the Law altogether. Paul had spoken in such vehement terms against the Law that it is not surprising if some of his converts, for example, the Corinthians, were inclined to take his statements about freedom a little too literally. If one was set free from the Law, did this not mean that one was set free from the ethical demands of the Law, as well as from its requirements about circumcision and sacrifice and food taboos? This, too, was an entirely logical course. One can see how it was that Paul's understanding of the gospel led to two such different misunderstandings. If the Law had been shown up as ineffective, then away with the Law; if the Law was understood as pointing forward to Christ, then the teaching of the Law must be obeyed. No doubt Paul was accused from either flank of wanting to eat his cake and have it. And perhaps to some extent the charge was true. Paul argues that the Law had been unable to do what it promised, i.e., to give men life; yet he uses it as the basis for all his own theological arguments, and maintains that the promises of the Law are in fact fulfilled in Christ. He tells the Galatians that they must not put themselves under the commands of the Law—meaning circumcision and other relevant observances; but when he comes to spell out what living in Christ means, he tends to do so in terms of ethical commands taken from the Law. Paul walks a tightrope in his theological explorations; he holds in tension two experiences which have to be given their due place; on the one hand, continuity with the past—with his Jewish heritage, the Old Testament scriptures, and the belief that God had been guiding his people in past ages: on the other, the exciting experience of the present—his belief that God was at work in Christ. Past and present, tradition and experience, needed to be balanced. The whole of the New Testament reflects the tension between these two factors, between the Jewish inheritance and Christian experience; and it is fascinating to compare the various ways in which the writers of the New Testament coped with this tension. It is a tension which has continued throughout the Church history and to some extent continues to cause problems. I suppose most of us today would use the Old Testament in a way which is a watered down version of Paul's approach—sometimes negatively, sometimes positively; it is arguable that we, too, are wanting to eat our cake and have it. The Church has never really solved the problem of the canon. And today the problem of the tension between old and new emerges in a different form—the problem of the tension between traditions from the past, and a Christian experience which seems to demand a new kind of language.

But let us return to Paul on his tightrope. If he succeeded in walking it securely (and perhaps he was not always successful), one wonders how many of his converts were able to follow his example, and how many toppled off! Clearly there were many who could not balance between continuity with the past and new experience, and who either returned to what Paul described as slavery, or accepted the freedom which he offered them with such enthusiasm that it became an excuse for licence. One wonders whether Paul was aware—at first!—of the problems which his gospel of freedom from the Law might cause in a pagan environment. For him, a conscientious Jew by upbringing and training, certain modes of behaviour were normal, instinctive; it would not have occurred to him to steal his neighbour's cattle, or to commit adultery, or become involved in a drunken brawl. Jewish converts to Christianity were unlikely to have been led into wild excesses of immorality by their new-found faith in Jesus as Lord; to them, it would have been natural to continue to see the demands of the Law as a way of expressing their obedience to God. For them, the danger was that they might cling too tightly to past tradition, and not experience the new liberation of faith in Christ. In some ways it was much easier for pagans to break with the past when they became Christians. They discarded their old religions, and with it their gods and religious customs. Yet they continued to live in a pagan environment, surrounded by those who still worshipped the old gods, practised the old traditions and lived accordingly to the old morality. Without the advantage of a Jewish background which linked belief in God with ethical behaviour, it was by no means obvious to them all that their new-found faith demanded certain modes of behaviour. Paul therefore found it necessary to spell out to them what he meant by living in Christ. But first he had to explain why certain kinds of behaviour are *incompatible* with living in Christ.

76

We have seen that Paul can speak about Christ dying on our behalf. He also turns the idea the other way round, and speaks of our dying with Christ. Christ dies, not as our substitute, but as our representative; 'one has died,' says Paul, 'therefore all have died'. Paul uses a variety of verbs compounded with the preposition 'with': we have died with Christ, been crucified with Christ, have risen with Christ, been glorified with Christ. But this is not just religious language, or a dramatic way of describing baptism. For Paul, our old way of life—what we were—is past and done with. We have a new life, in Christ. This is why Paul can transfer his parallel between Adam and Christ, used when he was talking about redemption, to his instructions about Christian behaviour. Put off the old man, he says; put the old man to death. You have done with that kind of living, for it belongs to life in Adam. Put on the new man, i.e., Jesus Christ, and live in him; be conformed to the pattern of his life; let your own lives demonstrate the behaviour which belongs to him. For Paul, ethics is always rooted in theology. It is no accident that the form of every Pauline letter is a section of theology followed by a section on ethics—not because he *divides* the two, but because the one leads to the other; ethics depends on theology. It is not a separate compartment of existence but the inevitable working out of what life in Christ is all about.

This is why in dealing with particular ethical problems, Paul almost always goes back to first principles. Faced with the problem of how Christians should behave in a difficult situation, Paul's method is to apply basic theological principles. This is why the *way* in which Paul deals with ethical problems may well be worth studying even when the problems themselves seem totally remote from the modern world. It is because he applies his understanding of the gospel to each situation that we find Christological statements popping up in what might seem like improbable contexts. When Paul is trying to persuade the Corinthians to make a weekly collection—to set aside, week by week, a monetary contribution for others in the Church—he gives a variety of reasons, but the most memorable advice is that they ought to remember the grace of our Lord Jesus Christ, how though he was rich, yet for their sakes he became poor, that by his poverty they might become rich.[3] We have already explored the meaning of this summary of the gospel. Now we see how Paul is using it; it is the basis of an appeal to the Corinthians to behave like Christ. If they are in him, then they should be demonstrating in their lives the characteristics of the life of Christ; the same principle of riches for others resulting from self-giving should be seen in them as in Christ. This is what living in Christ means.

It means, as Paul puts it in Philippians 2, having the mind of Christ. Here again we have one of the most famous summaries of the gospel in the Pauline letters, and it is a passage which we have looked at already, because, like the Corinthian summary, it describes how Christ shared in what we are. 'Have this mind in you, which was in Christ—who, being in the form of God, thought it no robbery to be equal with God, but emptied himself, taking the form of a slave . . .' Once again, we see how Paul uses this summary; the Philippians, he says, are to have the same mind, Christ's mind. The context of the letter shows the relevance of the particular description of Christ's action. Just as the Corinthians were apparently somewhat ungenerous, and needed to be stirred into generosity by Paul's appeal, so there was some wrangling going on among some of the members of the Philippian church, each of them standing on his or her rights. Paul's appeal is to be generous in dealing with fellow-believers, considering others better than oneself, giving place to others—following the example of Christ.

Appeals to imitate the example of others are all very well, but do not in the long run provide the power which is necessary to put the appeal into effect. Philippians 2:5 is an interesting example of the way in which changing exegesis

[3] 2 Corinthians 8:9

78

has influenced the translation of the passage. There is a problem in this verse, because in English it is necessary to supply a verb in the second clause where none is required in the original Greek. The translators of the Authorised Version solved the problem by repeating the verb 'to be' which they had used to translate the imperative with which the sentence begins: 'Let this mind be in you, which was also in Christ Jesus.' Christians were to imitate Jesus—to behave as he behaved. The Revisers understand the passage in the same way. But, argued the commentators, this passage is not an appeal to imitate Christ—that is much too shallow a view of what Paul has in mind. The first verb in the verse is in fact the verb 'to think' and this is the verb which we need to supply in the second half of the verse. The Philippians are to think among themselves as they think in Christ Jesus. So we find the New English Bible presumably trying to convey something of this sense with the translation: 'Let your bearing towards one another arise out of your life in Christ Jesus.' The phrase 'in Christ' is being given the usual sense which it has in Paul—it refers, not to the mind of the earthly Jesus . . . but to the way of thinking which belongs to those who are in Christ. The Revised Standard Version hovers between these two interpretations by giving us a translation which can be interpreted in either way: 'Have this mind among yourselves, which you have in Christ Jesus'.

I am not sure whether the translators of the Revised Standard Version are sitting on the fence, because they cannot make up their minds which interpretation is right, or whether they are wanting to keep their cake and eat it, because they think that *both* are right! I, at any rate, want to do the latter. I think it is true that Paul is not simply appealing to the example of Christ, and urging the Philippians to follow it. Christian living is not a case of following in the master's footsteps, like the page stumbling in the snow behind Good King Wenceslas. It is not a question of trying to copy a pattern: rather it is a case of being

79

conformed to that pattern, because they are in Christ. 'Let your bearing towards one another arise out of your life in Christ Jesus'; they are already in Christ—already part of the Christian community—so the behaviour and thought-patterns which are proper to that community must be demonstrated in those who belong to it. But notice that Paul does not say simply 'in Christ' here but 'in Christ *Jesus*', almost as though he wanted to remind us that what he is describing is not a general description of the kind of thing which ought to be seen in the Christian community, but is the direct result of the living and the dying of a particular person. Of course the Philippians cannot simply imitate Christ! But the behaviour which must characterize their lives is dependent on the behaviour which characterized Jesus; there is a link between the mind of Christ, seen in the gospel events, and the mind which they now have 'in Christ.' Christians are, as it were, caught up into the life of Christ; the mind and attitude which belonged to him now belong to those who are in him, who share his resurrection life. His life overflows into those who are in him.

But if this is the idea which Paul is trying to express, then the pattern which applied to Christ ought also to apply to those who are in him. Christ became poor, in order that he might make us rich. We have already seen that Paul extends this to the Corinthians. They, too, ought to use their riches (such as they are) to make those who are poor rich. I have suggested already that what Paul says in Philippians 2 about Jesus humbling himself and taking the form of a slave, and being found in the fashion of a man, has its logical conclusion in the following chapter, where Paul speaks of our bodies of humiliation being transformed and fashioned to be like his. But in that chapter Paul also speaks of the way in which he has been content to discard everything that he prized in order to gain Christ, and be found in him, sharing his sufferings, becoming like him in death, in order to share in his resurrection. Once again, Christ's self-giving and death are not seen as a substitute for ours,

80

but as a pattern to which the Christian is to be conformed; we shall be glorified with him, says Paul in Romans[4], provided we suffer with him as well. And just as in Christ's case, the life given away led to a life which overflowed for the benefit of others, so with Paul, his sufferings are used by God for the benefit of others. The principle of life through death, riches through poverty, joy through sorrow, glory through shame, is something which extends beyond the relationship of Christ and those who are in Christ, to the relationship between one believer and another. Life in Christ means the working out of the pattern which was seen in Christ.

It was the Corinthians' failure to realize that they were called to participate in the sufferings of Christ that led them to suppose that they could by-pass the shame and suffering and go straight for honour and glory; they thought of their Christian experience in terms of life, joy and glory alone. The result was that they expected honour and position for themselves, and despised their somewhat disreputable apostle, who embarrassed them by his apparent lack of success, by being persecuted by his enemies, punished by Jewish authorities, imprisoned by state officials, hounded from one city to another, and on top of everything else by being repeatedly shipwrecked—a sign, perhaps, of divine displeasure in addition to his other afflictions. By expecting status and honour the Corinthians demonstrate, in Paul's judgment, their complete failure to understand the Cross: Christ's suffering and shame are not meant as a substitute for ours—on the contrary, they are the pattern to which Christians are called to be conformed.

In other words, life in Christ is not, as Paul sees it, simply a case of being on the receiving end of God's redemptive act; nor is it simply a question of Christians modelling their lives on the example of Christ. Rather it is a sharing in the experience of Christ—in the dying and rising, the giving and receiving—and this means it is also a sharing in the

[4] Romans 8:17

81

redemptive mission of Christ. This is an idea which emerges clearly in 2 Corinthians, when Paul describes his relationship with the Corinthians: Paul has been afflicted, and the Corinthians comforted, i.e., they have shared in the comfort which has come to Paul in his afflictions; the comfort has, as it were, overflowed from Paul's experience into theirs. 'Death is at work in us, and life in you', says Paul—but once again, this is not just a simple exchange; 'we are always being given up to death for Jesus' sake, so that the life of Jesus may be revealed in our mortal bodies.' Jesus died and was raised to life, and the life pours over into others; they, in turn, die with him—and they, too, become sources of life for others. To live in Christ is to share in the death and resurrection of Christ. This is why Christians cannot retreat from the world to live in a holy huddle on their own; if they are in Christ, they share in his mission to the world.

It is not surprising if Paul uses creation language to describe this experience of resurrection: 'if anyone is in Christ, there is a new creation'. Life has begun again—mankind has begun again, dependent this time not upon Adam, but upon Christ. But this means that the world itself—put out of joint by Adam's sin, ought to be sharing in the restoration. And this, of course, is Paul's great hope for the future: the universe groans and travails, waiting in expectation for its restoration to God's original plan and purpose. In the meantime, Paul maintains that the creative power of God seen at work in Christ is more powerful than all the powers of evil which have dominated the world because of man's weakness; he does not deny their existence, but he is confident that none of them is able to separate the believer from Christ; those who are in Christ share in the victory which brings life out of death and defeats evil with blessing.

SIX

Dying, and behold we live

I began this book by pointing out some of the difficulties involved in understanding Paul and in trying to build a comprehensive picture of his theology. As we have gone along, we have collected a few more problems—the result of trying to eavesdrop on one end of a telephone conversation, when we do not really understand the situation being discussed, and are not familiar with the language being used. In this final chapter I want to see if I can pick up some of the loose ends with which I am left; I hesitate to suggest that I may be able to weave them into a pattern—for if I did, I might well be producing a pattern which Paul himself would not recognize! But at least we can have a look at these loose ends and size up the problem.

Paul's understanding of the gospel is, as we have seen, focused on the figure of Christ. It is here that we see the saving activity of God revealed. The righteousness of God is demonstrated in Christ, because God's act of vindication and man's act of obedience meet in one figure. I have already suggested that Paul found the term 'Son of God' particularly appropriate for conveying this idea of Christ as the one who expresses both God's saving purpose for mankind, and mankind's obedient response to God. But it raises also for us questions about Paul's Christology. How did he understand the relationship between God and Christ? And what of the role of the Holy Spirit? Can we find trinitarian belief in Paul, or is this something which emerges at a later period in the Church's history?

Needless to say, Paul provides us with no neat answers to these questions—probably because they would not have occurred to him. If we try to force him into a pattern, we run up against all sorts of difficulties. And just when we think he may be answering one of our questions, the evidence tends to be infuriatingly ambiguous. There is no passage, for example, where Paul calls Christ 'God'. Or is there? One or two passages might perhaps be interpreted in this way, but with no degree of certainty.[1] Yet Paul applies to Christ various Old Testament passages which refer to Yahweh[2]—and he uses the Greek equivalent of this divine name, the Lord, of both God and Christ. Just to confuse us, on one occasion he tells us that the Lord is the Spirit.[3] As for the Spirit, this is spoken of both as the Spirit of God and as the Spirit of the Son. The Spirit who lives in believers is the Spirit of God who raised Christ from the dead[4]; but it is the Spirit of the Son who has been sent into our hearts, enabling us to call God 'Father'.[5] If Paul's usage of terms seems unsystematic, it is because his theology arises out of his experience. The terms which he uses express the ways in which he has known God. The closest thing to a trinitarian formula, for example, is found in the final verse of 2 Corinthians, where Paul prays that the Corinthians may experience the love of God, the grace of the Lord Jesus, and the fellowship of the Holy Spirit. The words which he uses here are appropriate to the ways in which Christians do in fact experience God—the love of God, the grace of the Lord Jesus, the fellowship of the Spirit. To ask Paul whether he believed in the trinity would have been an unfair question. The doctrine developed later in an attempt to spell out what in Paul's time was only experienced. And though Paul may not supply answers to our theological questions, this seems to me to be no loss, for what he gives us is theology which is lived and experienced rather than formulated.

By the time we reach the letter to the Ephesians, written

[1] The relevant passages are Romans 9:5 and Titus 2:13. The latter is unlikely to have been written by Paul himself.

[2] E.g., Isaiah 45:23, used of God in Romans 14:11, is applied to Christ in Philippians 2:10 f.

[3] 2 Corinthians 3:17

[4] Romans 8:11

[5] Galatians 4:6

probably by someone who was an admirer of Paul rather than by Paul himself, doctrinal statements begin to be somewhat more developed. The opening verses of Ephesians 1 sum up what God has done for us. The passage falls naturally into a trinitarian pattern, as the author describes what God the Father of our Lord Jesus Christ has done for us in Christ, and the way in which those who are in Christ have received the Holy Spirit. The trinitarian pattern is probably unconscious; it emerges naturally in this attempt to sum up the redeeming activity of God experienced by Christians.

The beginning of this redemptive activity is traced back in this passage to a time before the foundation of the world. God chose us in Christ before the world was founded. Here we have the notion that we pre-existed—if only as an idea in the mind of God—from before the beginning of time. This brings us back to the problem of pre-existence which we postponed earlier. Does Paul think of Christ as pre-existent? And if so, what would he have understood by this? Here, too, our evidence is scanty. It is to be found in passages which we have already looked at where Paul speaks of the way in which God redeemed men and women through his Son. He sent his Son, he tells us a couple of times—does that mean that the Son was pre-existent? It is by no means clear that this idea was in Paul's mind; commentators poring over Paul's words might perhaps think that this is what, logically, they imply, but it is unlikely that the question ever occurred to Paul himself. But you will remember that in some of the passages we looked at earlier, when we were thinking of the idea of Christ becoming what we are, the emphasis shifted from the activity of God to the idea that Christ himself willingly shared it. A good example of this is found if we compare Romans 8:32 with Galatians 2:20: God is on our side, and gave up his own Son for us; Christ loved me, and gave himself up for me. The same verb is used in both verses; in one the action is that of God, in the other it is that of his

Son. Similarly, there are a couple of passages in which the emphasis is on the activity of Christ, where the idea is perhaps pushed back into the pre-existent life of Christ, though Paul's precise meaning is by no means clear. These are the passages which we looked at in the last chapter—2 Corinthians 8:9, which speaks of Christ becoming poor, and Philippians 2, where Christ is described as emptying himself. But you will remember that the context of both these passages was an appeal to be like Christ, to be conformed to his way of life. And you will remember also the significant way in which Paul continues the argument. In 2 Corinthians 8:9, the climax of the sentence is not about Christ but about Christians—the statement that by his impoverishment we become rich; and the meaning of Philippians 2 is worked out by Paul in the following chapter, where we find that we are conformed to Christ's glory. So that Christ's pre-existence, in so far as Paul describes it, is not a metaphysical condition, but a statement about man's destiny. Christ is what man was meant to be in God's intention; the redemption which he achieves in us is that we, by being in him, become what humanity was meant to be. He was rich—and became poor—in order to make others rich; he was in the form of God, and took human form, in order that we might be conformed to his glory. The pre-existent Christ expresses God's purpose for us.

It is perhaps not surprising to discover, if we turn to Jewish writings of the period, that the notion of pre-existence is used there in order to express the idea of God's purpose; God's plan for mankind is laid up in heaven—it pre-exists its realization on earth. The Law, for example, is said to have been with God from before the creation. God's plan and purpose are no afterthought. Had we asked Paul the question, 'What was the pre-existent Christ doing before the incarnation?', I do not think he would have understood the question. We must allow Paul to answer his own questions and not ours. The significant difference between the notion of pre-existence in Jewish thought and

86

in Paul's theology is that for Paul, the predetermined plan and purpose of God are expressed in a person—in Christ—and not in the Law. He is presented as the blueprint for mankind.

The idea of pre-existence raises the question of time, which leads us in turn to the notion of eschatology. It is obvious that Paul wrote—that indeed he lived and thought—against what I have already termed an eschatological backcloth; but his understanding of world history was so different from ours that we tend to ignore it. In doing so, of course, we inevitably distort what he is saying. Paul assumes a story of human salvation which begins with God's creation of a perfect universe; in which man's fall leads to corruption throughout the universe, and is then reversed by the death and resurrection of Christ. The end of history will be a restoration of the universe to God's original plan and purpose. Paradise Lost is one half of the story, Paradise Regained the other, with Christ's Cross and resurrection as the great turning point. We have seen already how Paul's imagery assumes this pattern; so does his whole understanding of man's situation. Humanity has become subject to sin and death because of Adam's sin: men and women have lost the glory which belonged to Adam. There are many rabbinic legends which describe the glory of Adam before the Fall. When he spoke face to face with God in the garden of Eden, he naturally reflected the glory of God; he gave glory to God, and reflected glory himself. Since Adam, no man has spoken face to face with God; Moses indeed caught a glimpse of the backside of God's glory as he passed by on Mount Sinai—and look what happened to him! The glory which shone from his face was so powerful that the people of Israel could not stand the sight, and Moses had to keep his head covered. But now in Christ, says Paul, the situation is entirely different. Christ is what Adam was meant to be, the image of God himself [6]; he reflects the glory of God, far more effectively

[6] Colossians 1:15; 3:10

than Moses ever did, and Christians who look at Christ are themselves set alight with glory[7]; they, too, are restored to what Adam was meant to be—or at least they will be, when the restoration of the universe is complete. And not only is mankind to be restored to the glory which Adam lost, the universe itself is to be restored, for in Paul's view the fact that creation has gone awry—been subjected to bondage—is the result also of Adam's sin.[8]

Now this eschatological backcloth against which Paul projects man's salvation consists of three stages: there is the world as God created it, and as Adam enjoyed it; there is the fallen world, which resulted from Adam's sin, and in which we all live; and there is the world restored to what it ought to be—a world which remains as a future hope, even though it exists already *in nuce* in Christ. This three-fold division of history seems to me just as important for Paul's way of thinking as the so-called three-decker universe, which thinks of space in terms of up there, here, and down there—heaven, earth and hell. It is now commonly recognized that the first-century notion of space needs to be demythologized; we no longer think of God as being 'up there'—though somewhat surprisingly, in searching for an alternative image, theologians tend to plump for the idea of God as the ground of our being, which is simply to substitute one spatial image for another. But this spatial notion of earth as the middle of a sandwich, in between the powers up there and the powers down there, is matched by the temporal notion of earth as the middle of another sandwich, in between time back there—in the blissful time before the Fall—and time beyond the Eschaton, when everything will be put to rights. Ought we not to demythologize this metaphor also? For if we know now that God is not to be located 'up there', we also know that Paradise was never experienced in some prehistoric period in the Garden of Eden. And of course, to some extent, this is precisely what

[7] 2 Corinthians 3:7–4:6
[8] Romans 8:18–25

88

we do. We no longer think of the Fall of man as taking place at a particular moment of time; we do not imagine that the world was once perfect, and that it is man's sin which has caused nature to be red in tooth and claw. The book of Genesis may see death as the direct result of Adam's disobedience, and regard the Flood as a divine judgment on human sin, but we no longer regard death or disaster as an unnatural punishment. Like Paul himself in Romans 1, we have demythologized Adam. But what about the rest of the picture? What do we do with the eschatological hope—which looks for a restoration of mankind to what Adam once was?

The answer, usually, is that we do our best to forget it! Apart from those who still look for a literal fulfilment of the promise that Christ will come again in glory, and earth be set to rights, most of us are embarrassed by the eschatological hope for a restoration of this world; we do not know how to deal with the idea that creation itself will be redeemed. But if we have demythologized the notion of man's fall, must we not also demythologize the corresponding idea of his restoration? And if, in thinking about the biblical spatial image of a three-decker universe, we have discarded the notion of space, and see the image as an expression of the relationship between man and God, should we not discard the notion of time from the biblical image of an End which is a return to a beginning? Is not this biblical view of time a way of expressing an idea which we found in the notion of Christ's pre-existence—the idea of God's purpose for mankind, set out, as it were, before the beginning of history, and lying ahead of us, beyond the end of history, as the goal at which we should aim?

Paul himself sets out his understanding of history in terms of a linear view of history—history moving from an original Paradise through the Fall to a recreation in Christ and a final restoration which will be a restoration to the original glory. Yet even for Paul, this scheme does not really work; for the future is continually breaking into the present. Eschatology belongs, by definition, to the end of time. Yet in the New Testament we find that eschatology belongs to the present; it may not be realized—but it is certainly in the process of realization. What belongs to the End of time—judgment, death and resurrection—has already taken place, even though it must take place again. Reconciliation with God—and all the consequences of that reconciliation—is something which Christians already experience, and yet it is something which they will experience in even greater depth in the future. The Spirit of God, who is the symbol of the final age, is already here, and yet he is here only as an *arrabon*[9]—a Greek word which means a first instalment; he is the guarantee of something still to come. You have already died, says Paul, already been raised; death has been defeated; you have died to sin, and so you cannot live under its power.[10] It is possible that at an early stage Paul did in fact believe that Christians would not have to die again, but he soon had to recognize that death was not yet finally defeated; and the behaviour of some of his converts, the Corinthians, for example, must have convinced him that sin was still very much alive and kicking. The powers of chaos and disorder have been defeated—and yet they continue to batter mankind.

Paul is not alone, of course, in maintaining that the End is here and yet not here; that the future is somehow pressing into the present. Exactly the same eschatological tension is seen in the gospels, in the sayings about the Kingdom of God. It is at hand—it is both present and future; it has burst upon Jesus's contemporaries, and yet it is still to come. Those who have eyes to see can see it, while to others it remains hidden from sight; it is both here and *not* yet here. I wonder whether it is not precisely in this paradox of the eschatological tension between what is and what is not that we must look for the answer to my problem about the way

[9] 2 Corinthians 1:22; 5:5; Ephesians 1:14
[10] Romans 6:2–4; Colossians 2:12; 3:1

in which Paul depicts the hope for the future as a return to Paradise—as a winding-up of history. It is true that his thought is projected against what I have described as an eschatological backcloth, which links redemption closely with a linear view of history, so that he sees our redemption as a movement towards a final sorting-out and putting to rights. Yet at the same time he has projected onto this backcloth another view of redemption, which superimposes the future upon the present; a view in which it is not so much a case of event A being followed by event B, as of event A and event B illuminating one another. The former approach might be called histori-cal—or perhaps, somewhat paradoxically, mythologi-cal—and the second theological. Let me illustrate. Perhaps the best example of what I mean is to be found, not in Paul's letters, but in the Fourth Gospel. It is well-known that whereas in the Synoptic gospels we have a number of passion predictions which speak of the necessity for the Son of man to die, followed by the promise that he will be raised from the dead, and other sayings which speak of the future glorification of the Son of man, following the present period of humiliation, what we have in John is somewhat different. There we find sayings about the Son of man being glorified by his death; although in the course of his passion narrative John describes first the crucifixion of Jesus and then the resurrection appearances, in his theological com-mentary on what is happening in the discourses he seems to have fused the idea of shame with that of glory, the fact of death with the experience of resurrection. The Christian looks at the Cross from the viewpoint of one who knows its consequences—and sees it, therefore, not only as an instrument of death but as a display of glory. Paul, I think, does something rather similar—though of course he does it in his own way; for him, too, death and resurrection, shame and glory, sorrow and joy, are superimposed. But Paul interprets not only the Cross of Christ in this way; since Christians are crucified with Christ, this fusion of death and life, shame and glory, sorrow and joy, is experienced by them also.

Christian hope has often been expressed in terms which are almost entirely future: in terms, that is, of a future glory which is detached from the present; as a recompense to make up for present suffering; as pie in the sky when you die—to make up for the lack of pie here and now; as a future setting right of earthly iniquities. On this view, there is no real continuity with present experience—rather there is a break. Paul, it seems to me, is far more profound. The process of restoration does not belong only to the future; it belongs to the present as well. Christians are already glorified—even though their glory may not be obvious to the world at large! They are already being changed from one degree of glory to another; already they are conformed to the pattern of Christ—which means that they are already sharing in his life as well as in his death. The power of God which raised Christ from death and which raises Christians to life does not belong only to the past and to the future; it is something which is experienced in the present, in the lives of those who are in Christ. It is not a case of experiencing sorrow and suffering and death today, and joy and glory and life tomorrow. Rather it is a case of already experiencing a joy which works through sorrow, a glory found in shame, a wholeness which comes through suffering, a life which emerges from death. In *Through the Looking Glass*, Alice is told that she can have jam every other day—which means jam yesterday and jam tomorrow, but never jam today. Paul, it would seem, is in disagreement; logically, jam may belong to yesterday and tomorrow; yet paradoxically it is available today, for those who are in Christ.

Yet *is* it illogical? If our thinking is dominated by the eschatological hope, yes. On a linear view of history as the unfolding of God's plan of salvation, restoration belongs to the future. But the paradox of the Christian faith is that the Eschaton is here, in Christ, and is symbolized in the Cross, where life and death, joy and sorrow, suffering and healing coalesce. Restoration is no longer just a future hope but a present experience—and what we experience is in many ways more real to us than what we hope for. It is unfortunate that traditional theology has placed so much emphasis on the last judgment and the final sorting out of history that it has tended to play down the present experience of resurrection as a valid way of interpreting this theme of restoration. Yet there is no doubt that this theme of present restoration is an important one in the New Testament—not only in Paul's letters, but in the gospels in particular, where salvation confronts men and women here and now in the person of Jesus Christ. Redemption is to be experienced here and now, and is to be found in the ordinary everyday life once shared by him.

There are, I think, two obvious ways in which this present experience of redemption is symbolized and proclaimed and Paul refers to both of them; they are baptism and the eucharist. For Paul, baptism is a dying with Christ. No doubt in his day the candidate for baptism would have been submerged beneath the water and would have emerged from the water—a much more vivid portrayal of the idea of death, burial and resurrection than the timid application of a few drops of warm water to a baby's forehead with which we are familiar. For Paul, baptism is an incorporation into Christ's death, not into a respected social community. In Jewish thought water often symbolizes the powers of chaos which can so easily overwhelm a man. The Christian, joined to Christ, is overwhelmed by death and disaster—but rises triumphant. The ritual symbolizes Christian experience; at one and the same time it looks back to the historical dying of Jesus and forwards to the hope of future resurrection. But the dying and the rising coalesce at this point in the present. Baptism symbolizes the believer's experience here and now, of new life opening up at the very moment that one dies to what is past.

The eucharist also looks back to the death of Christ; it is a portrayal of the events at the Last Supper, which was itself interpreted as an exposition of Christ's death. But this, too, looks forward—it is seen as a foretaste of the messianic banquet, a dramatic way of speaking of the hope for the future. Yet once again, looking both forwards and backwards, it is very much an expression of a present experience—the experience of the living presence of Christ. Believers are once again united with the death and resurrection of Christ. In these two symbolic representations of the Cross, baptism and eucharist, we see that experiences which we tend to think of as opposites—life and death, joy and sorrow, glory and shame, health and suffering—are in fact fused together. This is the paradox of the Cross itself, the paradox of life which comes through death. It has never been summed up better than by Paul himself, when he described himself as 'always carrying in the body the death of Jesus, so that the life of Jesus may also be manifested in our bodies. For while we live we are always being given up to death for Jesus' sake, so that the life of Jesus may be manifested in our mortal flesh. So death is at work in us, but life in you.' [11] Paul has made Christ's experience of death and resurrection his own. No wonder, then, that he dares to speak of Christians reflecting the glory of God, as they are transformed into Christ's own image. For in Paul's view, experiences which are normally assumed to be mutually exclusive are found, in Christ, to overlap: the glory of God is revealed in shame; his power is demonstrated through weakness; his wisdom is disclosed in foolishness; his resources are discovered in total emptiness. In stressing the Christian hope for future resurrection, glory and reward, it may be that Christians have sometimes tended to overlook this other aspect of the gospel, which finds glory, power and resurrection within present experiences of shame, weakness and death. This is the ultimate scandal of the Cross; but it is a scandal which Paul has fully grasped when he speaks of God's power being perfected in weakness, and declares[12]: 'It is when I am weak that I am strong'. Paul's

[11] 2 Corinthians 4:10–12, R.S.V.

94

'strength' in this case is not hope for the future, but is experienced through weakness itself; he finds significance for his suffering, not in a hope of future restoration, but in a present experience of God's power.

It is natural for men to expect God to reveal himself in glory, wisdom and power. Paul himself uses all those terms to describe God's activity; but he reminds us that in the divine pattern these ideas may well all be turned on their heads, so that men fail to see God at work. It is all too easy to look for future glory in the heavens and ignore the glory under one's feet, but if God reveals himself supremely in the degradation of the Cross, then there is no human situation in which he may not be found.

[12] 2 Corinthians 12:9 f.

Most readers of the New Testament have a clearly defined attitude towards the Apostle Paul, and frequently it is a negative one. In many instances, their opinion is based upon a combination of misunderstanding, prejudice, and a failure to recognize that Paul wrote for an age very different from our own. We naturally tend to interpret Paul from our own standpoint, forgetting that the situation of the early Christian community was totally unlike that of Christians today. The result is that Paul is not allowed to speak for himself, but is expected to answer our questions—and blamed when he fails to do so to our satisfaction.

This introduction to the Church's first great theologian does not attempt to produce a systematic account of his theology. Indeed, it begins from the recognition that such an attempt is impossible: all we have on which to base our reconstruction of Paul's thought is part of his correspondence with some of his churches, and usually we have to guess at what these letters presuppose. All too often, readers of Paul make the mistake of treating the Pauline material as a corpus of teaching, comprehensive in its range and timeless in its relevance. *A Preface to Paul* attempts to show that we distort Paul's meaning when we treat him in this way, but that by trying to put ourselves imaginatively into his situation we can begin to understand how the Apostle's thought can still be relevant to us today.

Morna Hooker, who has taught in King's College, London, and the University of Oxford, is now Lady Margaret's Professor of Divinity in the University of Cambridge, and a Fellow of Robinson College, the most recently established of the Cambridge Colleges.